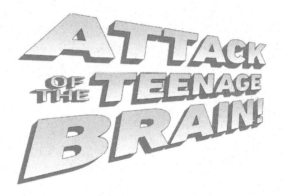

UNDERSTANDING AND SUPPORTING
THE WEIRD AND WONDERFUL ADOLESCENT LEARNER

ATTACK OF THE TEENAGE BRAIN!

JOHN **MEDINA**

Arlington, Virginia USA

2800 Shirlington Road, Suite 1001 • Arlington, VA 22206 USA
Phone: 800-933-2723 or 703-578-9600 • Fax: 703-575-5400
Website: www.ascd.org • E-mail: member@ascd.org
Author guidelines: www.ascd.org/write

Deborah S. Delisle, *Executive Director;* Stefani Roth, *Publisher;* Genny Ostertag, *Director, Content Acquisitions;* Susan Hills, *Acquisitions Editor;* Julie Houtz, *Director, Book Editing & Production;* Katie Martin, *Editor;* Thomas Lytle, *Senior Graphic Designer;* Mike Kalyan, *Director, Production Services;* Cynthia Stock, *Typesetter;* Kyle Steichen, *Senior Production Specialist*

PAPERBACK ISBN: 978-1-4166-2549-0   ASCD product #118024   n3/18
PDF E-BOOK ISBN: 978-1-4166-2551-3; see Books in Print for other formats.
Quantity discounts are available: e-mail programteam@ascd.org or call 800-933-2723, ext. 5773, or 703-575-5773. For desk copies, go to www.ascd.org/deskcopy.

Library of Congress Cataloging-in-Publication Data
Names: Medina, John, 1956- author.
Title: Attack of the teenage brain! : understanding and supporting the weird
    and wonderful adolescent learner / John Medina.
Description: Alexandria, VA USA : ASCD, 2018. | Includes bibliographical
    references and index.
Identifiers: LCCN 2017052703 (print) | LCCN 2017061526 (ebook) | ISBN
    9781416625513 (PDF) | ISBN 9781416625490 (pbk.)
Subjects: LCSH: Learning, Psychology of. | Adolescent psychology. | Executive
    functions (Neuropsychology) | Cognition in adolescence. |
    Teenagers–Education.
Classification: LCC LB1060 (ebook) | LCC LB1060 .M435 2018 (print) | DDC
    370.15/23–dc23
LC record available at https://lccn.loc.gov/2017052703

27 26 25 24 23   2 3 4 5 6 7 8 9 10 11 12

For Corinne Cruver
1929–2017

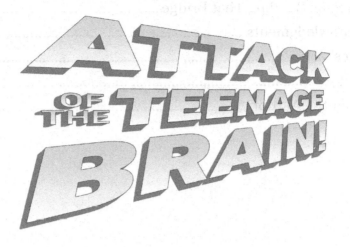

Introduction

Whether you're a parent interacting with one adolescent or a teacher interacting with many, you know the truth: teens can be hard to parent—and even harder to teach. When I drop the phrase "attack of the teenage brain," you nod knowingly. Perhaps the word "attack" even strikes you as an understatement.

I have a message for any adults currently sheltering in place as the Battle of Adolescence rages around you: you've come to the right book. We're going to talk about how to parent and teach teenagers, focusing primarily on education-related issues. We're also going to envision what a high school might look like if teen brain development were its optimal goal, and if we enlisted the cooperative efforts of parents and educators to help our challenging, sometimes infuriating, often weird, and genuinely wonderful kids get what they need as they fight their way toward adulthood.

Maybe you're too young to remember *Attack of the Teenage* anything. So let's kick things off with something still long in the tooth, but a bit more contemporary: a scene from *Star Trek III: The Search for Spock.*

It opens with stable, logical, good old Mr. Spock acting anything but stable, logical, or good-old. In the scene, he's a teenager, and we see him yelping at the moon and crying inconsolably—the Vulcan equivalent of stomping upstairs and slamming the bedroom door. We're told he is experiencing *pon farr,* a mysterious hormone surge that happens to beings of his race every seven years and must be sexually requited. Sounds to humans like a nightmarishly reoccurring puberty.

Mr. Spock is hardly alone in being bewildered by the seeming illogicality of sexual maturation, even if his struggles are constrained to a fictional once-every-seven-years itch. Whether in the 23rd century or the 21st, adolescence seems as inexplicable to the long-suffering human teens experiencing it as it does to long-suffering human adults witnessing it. To the research world, however, adolescence is neither inexplicable, illogical, nor unfamiliar. Puberty is as old as the Pleistocene and as recent as next week. I hope, in these pages, to use the sturdy tools of brain science to show just how much more familiar we are becoming with it, describing in detail the warp and woof of teenage brain development.

I am inviting you along on this journey not simply because the brain is an amazing place for teachers and parents to boldly go exploring, though it certainly is. This book has an explicit ulterior motive: I hope to show every teacher and parent on the planet why they should know and care about a specific cognitive gadget called executive function, and I hope to make the case for altering the educational landscape to help teens use their executive function skills more efficiently. This is, I believe, the missing link when it comes to improving secondary education.

I'll argue that more than any other single intervention, boosting executive function is a dependable method for improving teen academic achievement. And it also moonlights as the best way for frustrated parents to guide their *pon farr*–soaked charges. There is a constellation of peer-reviewed papers, mostly from the neurosciences, shedding light on the academic and social benefits of supporting executive function development.

The sunny light they radiate can warm adults who spend their days teaching teens on even the most behaviorally frigid days.

Getting to the Heart of the Brain

My first task in this book is to describe what executive function is; my second is to guide you through the mystery of why teens behave as they do; my third is to examine proven ways to enhance executive function and consider the consequences those findings have for education. Written primarily with teachers in mind, with an eye toward parents who can benefit as well, this book includes a fair amount of peer-reviewed behavioral psychology and neurobiology, which may sound scary or, worse, too esoteric to be truly useful.

Perhaps I can offer some reassurance. I am a developmental molecular biologist with research interests in the genetics of psychiatric disorders. I have spent most of my career as a private research consultant, working with companies ranging from biotech firms interested in the genes of schizophrenia to computer companies interested in anxiety. My participation in these advisory activities has led to many hours interacting with smart, highly motivated professionals whose last biology class occurred when they themselves underwent *pon farr*. So I promise to keep the jargon to a minimum, the concepts as clear as possible, and the prose liberally sprinkled with anecdotes and metaphors. I will insert the neurobiology where necessary, but always in pursuit of the goal of explaining executive function as clearly as I can.

Two Bits of Background

In support of this vow of clarity, I have two pieces of background information to share before we embark. The first concerns how scientists view the origins of human behavior.

We used to regularly engage in silly intellectual food fights about whether behaviors were caused by nature or by nurture, whether they were hardwired in human genes or softwired in the culture. We stopped fighting about this when our research told us we were using the wrong conjunction: it's not nature *or* nurture; it's nature *and* nurture.

To use a familiar example, you might be genetically programmed to achieve a certain height. Genes are proxy for nature here, under the regulatory control of human growth hormone. If you aren't fed properly during childhood, however, your growth may be permanently stunted. That's nurture, overriding any executive order your height hormone may try to issue. Both nature and nurture serve as chefs in this kitchen, and together, they dish out how tall you become. This duality is also very true of executive function, as I will explain later.

The second piece of background has to do with some frankly off-putting attitudes a few adults (not you, of course) have about teens. Some think adolescents are simply defective grown-ups, that there is something "wrong" with them when they act like horny aliens from Mars—or Vulcan. There is no question that adolescents aren't adults, but I hope to show that "defective" is hardly the right word to describe them. We'll discover that teen brains were genetically wired to perform specific functions, mostly related to solving problems of genetic diversity eons ago. If adolescents seem imperfect now, it's only because most of the obstacles their brains were wired to traverse no longer exist, and we haven't sojourned long enough in organized society for adolescent brains to get the memo. As the father of two teenagers, I can testify that teens make errors all the time. But there's a big difference between an error and a flaw.

If you can hang with me through all this, I promise to keep the neuroscience approachable and ensure that the intellectual load-bearing is done by peer-reviewed research. I promise to clearly explain how it relates to the teenagers in both the *Star*

Trek universe and in ours. And I'll draw it all together to show how we should tailor educational experiences to further teenagers' academic progress and social development.

Deal? If so, then I invite you to read on. We've got a whole galaxy of fascinating things to explore.

PART I

A BRIDGE OVER AN EDUCATIONAL CHASM

This part consists of a single problem-solving chapter. The pain point is one of the shames of American secondary education—our high schoolers' embarrassing international test scores. The remedy involves the cognitive gadget called executive function.

It's a "let's-roll-up-our" sleeves background for the rest of the book, which involves reimagining what a secondary educational experience might look like if optimizing teen brain development were its primary goal. And it all starts with a motorcycle, ridden by a man who didn't even finish high school.

1

ALL ABOUT
EXECUTIVE FUNCTION

You really question Darwin's assertion that only the fittest survive when you consider the antics of famed motorcycle daredevil Evel Knievel.

Back in 1974, Mr. Knievel got it into his head to jump the Snake River Canyon and have the attempt broadcast live on television. He announced that the stunt would occur near Twin Falls, Idaho, and that he'd jump from the canyon's south cliff to the north one, spanning a suicidal distance of nearly three-quarters of a mile. Because no Harley made has that kind of engine power, Knievel employed what was, for all intents and purposes, a two-wheeled rocket ship dubbed "The Skycycle." The spectacle ended up as one of the most famous nonevents in the checkered history of television, because the major networks refused to cover it.[1]

The good news was that Knievel survived. The bad news was that the jump was a bust. It began well enough, with the rocket roaring to life under the secure watch of the guy who built it, a former Naval rocket engineer. The Skycycle's parachute system wasn't as well behaved, unfortunately. It deployed early, almost as soon as the daredevil was airborne. Knievel drifted slowly, safely, to the canyon bottom, the wind blowing him back to the south side to a spot just below his point of origin. The Snake River Canyon would remain un-jumped for decades to come. When stuntman Eddie Braun accomplished the feat in 2016, he used a rocket-powered motorcycle designed by the son of the engineer who had developed Knievel's.

I'm going to use this jump by Knievel, a true American original, to describe something puzzling about another American original, the K–16 education system of the United States. To understand where the parallels lie, let's begin—perhaps unconventionally—at the end.

All Steak, No Sizzle

Much empirical evidence exists to support the self-serving, chest-puffing observation that higher education in the United States is the envy of the world. According to the research magazine *Nature,* nearly two-thirds of the world's highest-rated universities are American, including three of the top five.[2] The ratings may be deserved, if award-winning productivity is any measurement. More Nobel prizes have been given to U.S. scientists than to scientists in the next five represented countries *combined.*[3] The United States is especially strong in natural sciences Nobels; most are awarded to people who are (or were) employed by those top-ranked universities. Think of higher education in the United States as the terminating north cliff goal of Knievel's Snake River Canyon attempt, only with a happy ending.

In this metaphor, U.S. elementary schools are Knievel's starting point on the south side of the canyon, and they are similarly solid. The federal government (in the form of the National Assessment in Educational Progress, or NAEP) has been measuring school performance for decades, and its findings show that elementary schools are doing a pretty good job.[4] Although U.S. students are well-known to be underperformers in math, NAEP's findings show that our 4th graders' elementary math scores have increased 11 percent since the early 1970s. Reading scores have also improved—up 6 percent—in the same kids and over the same time span. American elementary schools' scores have been rising like yeast for years, and they are sufficiently robust, comparing favorably with schools in other countries.

So the two sides of the U.S. education "canyon" are in good shape. And if all you had to go on were these two data points, you'd think the system could be drawn as a statistically pleasing straight line that begins in quality elementary education and terminates at the pearly gates of Nobel Prize–festooned colleges.

Unfortunately, we're going to have to fasten our seat belts for the bumpy landing. A comparison of the scores of recent U.S. 17-year-olds to ones put up by 17-year-olds 40 years ago shows not one whit of improvement in math or reading. Teens today actually scored worse in science.[5] This means kids who were tested back when Pong was all the rage in video games achieved at basically the same levels as kids who grew up with Grand Theft Auto. The score differential for minority and disadvantaged youth shows even less progress.

This stasis is embarrassing, especially when U.S. language arts and math scores are compared with those of the rest of the world. Our 15-year-olds come in at a depressing #24 on the 2015 Programme for International Student Assessment (PISA). And for math, we are #36 out of 40.[6] Says noted psychologist Laurence Steinberg:

> Over the past forty years . . . and despite billions of dollars invested in school reform, there has been no improvement—none—in the academic proficiency of American high-school students. It's not just No Child Left Behind or Race to the Top that has failed our adolescents—*it's everything we have tried.*[7]

The italic emphasis is Steinberg's, but his pessimistic outlook is ours for the keeping.

And the bad news keeps rolling in, especially when our students try scampering up the far side of our educational chasm, banging on the doors of our lofty universities' admissions offices. To put it bluntly, many high school graduates just aren't ready for college. About 20 percent of starting freshmen spend time in the remedial education penalty box, and for an embarrassing reason: they didn't master the basics necessary to compete in world-class institutions.

It's even worse for students entering community colleges. About 50 percent need additional preparatory work,[8] except in California, where the figure is 80 percent.[9] And here's the weird thing: those Californian students in need of remediation graduated from their secondary schools with a *B* average, in the upper third of their classmates.[10] To make matters worse, many students who enroll in these "developmental courses" get stuck in them like a dinosaur in a tar pit. After six years, only 16 percent of the enrollees went on to get a degree.[11]

A Bridge Named Executive Function

These achievement data are ugly for sure, but they're not the whole story of U.S. education. There has been some recent improvement in grades and even graduation rates, especially for underserved populations. Still, that isn't much reassurance, especially when budgetary issues are taken into consideration. Higher graduation rates don't translate to much if you have to spend $3 billion a year—as we do—just to get kids up to scratch.[12] That kind of money should help make every kid an Eddie Braun, but we still have far too many Evel Knievels.

Obviously, we need to build a superior rocket-cycle—or even better, dispense with the quick fix altogether and build a bridge. That's what this book is all about: how to span the yawning academic chasm between strong elementary education and strong college education. We are going to use a modern neuroscientific understanding of teen brain development as the wood, hammer, and nail of the construction. This bridge even has a name, though it may sound more like something from a business school than a brain science concept: *executive function.*

Of *T. rex* and Marshmallows

Executive function (EF), defined in its baldest operational terms, is the ability to get something done—and not punch someone in the nose while doing it. That's a useful bit of oversimplification; to go more in depth, I'd like to start by explaining part of EF's origin story. To do that, I'll discuss the discovery of a dinosaur named Sue, then quickly move to marshmallows.

Obviously, I have some explaining to do.

Sue wasn't supposed to be discovered. The research team that found her had spent a summer in South Dakota digging for Cretaceous-era vegetarians and were packed up and ready to head home. Then a flat tire delayed the group's departure. While the tire was being fixed, self-taught paleontologist Sue Hendrickson wandered off for one last look around the geological neighborhood. It was an impulse that made her career. Spying a few curious-looking rocks at the foot of a nearby ridge, she looked up and noticed an even more curious protrusion jutting off the cliff's face.

The trip home could wait. Investigation of the protrusion revealed it to be a bone of the most intact fossilized *Tyrannosaurus rex* ever found. Almost 90 percent of skeleton was there (a paleontological find is considered monumental if just 50 percent of the bones are discovered). The famous fossil was named Sue, after her discoverer.[13]

This tip-of-the-iceberg phenomenon—that what looks at first to be a small finding can turn out to be a really big discovery—isn't limited to paleontology. You can see the same principle working in one of the most well-known experiments in the field of behavioral science, the one that eventually exposed the phenomenon of executive function. There, marshmallows took the place of digging equipment and fancy research-grade plasters.

Walter Mischel's legendary experiments at Stanford University in the late 1960s dealt with how children resisted temptation. In the experiment's most famous version, following a premise right out of TV's *Let's Make a Deal,* Mischel offered a series of 4-year-olds the choice of eating one tasty marshmallow immediately or waiting for 15 minutes—alone in the room, just the child and the uneaten marshmallow—after which he or she would receive two tasty marshmallows to eat.[14]

What happened could be difficult to watch. Most kids took the deal, though very few were able to follow through. Some kids ate the marshmallow within 30 seconds of the researcher leaving the room. Some valiantly resisted for a while, sitting on their hands, turning their backs to the marshmallow, or counting to 10 before caving in. A handful of supremely self-controlled subjects held out for the entire 15 minutes.

Records of each participant's results were stored for a long time while these kids percolated through the U.S. education system and into adulthood. Years later, Walter Mischel and his colleagues looked up hundreds of the young marshmallow experiment veterans to see how they had turned out.

What they found was both depressing and encouraging—and ultimately, groundbreaking. The kids who exhibited little self-control as 4-year-olds still exhibited little self-control years later. They achieved poorer grades and were less popular in school. They were more likely to be obese and more prone to drug abuse. The kids who held out for the whole 15 minutes also displayed extraordinary self-control years later. They got better grades in school and were more socially competent. They were physically fit and didn't abuse drugs. The data were fine-grained enough to conclude that the 15-minute holdouts scored, on average, 210 points higher on the SAT than the kids who caved within half a minute.[15]

The marshmallow experiment proved to be the Sue-bone protruding from the cliff. Further investigations into self-control revealed an entire body of behavioral tendencies that, as a group, were ultimately termed "executive function." This area of investigation is still very active, and for a very important reason: executive function correctly predicts aspects of a student's future. The accuracy of such statistical palm reading is about as rare in the behavioral sciences as prehistoric soft tissue is in paleontological finds. And one of the hottest areas of research involves the teen brain, with its hallmark developmental feature being the elaboration of executive function.

I will restate what I wrote in the Introduction—every teacher of teenagers should understand what executive function is and how it develops in adolescent brains—and underscore the urgency of such a claim by detailing how executive function comes by its predictive, prophetic power.

One Plus One Plus One Equals More

Despite the simplicity of its two-word label, executive function is tricky to define. It doesn't help that many scientists disagree on exactly what the darned thing is, managing to agree on just a few basic tenets. Fortunately, we can combine and recombine these few basic tenets to assemble a host of explanations for our external actions.

I am reminded of the purchasing habits my wife and I developed when we were in graduate school, and usually as broke as public television. In those poorer times, we were always on the lookout for a good deal on anything, down to the clothes we bought. My wife taught me the money-saving power of creating a mix-and-match wardrobe by buying a few elemental articles of clothing and combining them in different ways for different occasions. Similarly, EF encompasses a bewilderingly complex collection of human behaviors, but at its core are three simple, easily combined, and easily understood behavioral elements.

A Complex List

Let's look at an example of executive function in action.

Imagine your supervisor is yelling at you. You are startled, because he rarely yells at anyone. The ranting continues, and soon you want to punch him in the nose. But you don't. You engage in some emotional editing because you understand what the consequences of your desired action would be (loss of job security, impending assault charges) and you take responsibility for avoiding those consequences. You can perform this emotional editing because you're able to respond to situations as they occur, weighing advantages, managing risk, and imagining in advance what might happen if you choose violence. Your ability to respond in this fluid manner allows you to move from your present anger and into the future, if only for a few seconds, without losing track of your current circumstances.

As you begin to calm down, you contemplate your boss's outburst. You wonder what could have triggered his unusual behavior by trying to empathize, shifting your perspective to his. If you are successful, rationality returns, imposing order in your emotional life despite disparate inputs. Oddly enough, you can hold all these inputs and reactions in your brain's short-term memory banks long enough to complete the appeal to the better angels of your nature, and the situation comes to a nonviolent resolution.

According to most researchers, the complex wardrobe of behaviors that make up executive function boils down to mixing and matching a trio of foundational behaviors: (1) response inhibition, (2) cognitive flexibility, and (3) working memory.[16] Let's move from the analogy to the specifics of these concepts.

What Researchers Think

Here's one widely accepted definition of executive function:

> The executive functions are a set of processes that all have to do
> with managing oneself and one's resources in order to achieve
> a goal. It is an umbrella term for the neurologically-based skills
> involving mental control and self-regulation.[17]

Executive function's defining element is in the first sentence:
in order to achieve a goal. From a Darwinian perspective, the overall goal is survival. But since the brain decided to hang its evolutionary fate on fickle social interactions—a topic we'll take up in a
minute—it had to incorporate enough flexible gadgets to keep us
from killing ourselves. The definition thus consists of two hope-
lessly mixed metaphors: a combinatorial behavioral wardrobe
that allows you space to temper your urge to punch someone in
the nose with an awareness of the consequences of your actions.

The Neuroscience of Frank Capra

The movie *It's a Wonderful Life* came out in 1946, decades before
anyone had researched executive function. Yet one scene in
this classic movie depicts, in grayscale glory, one of the clearest
examples of adolescent EF I've ever seen.

Young George Bailey, while helping out the town pharmacist,
Mr. Gower, was supposed to deliver a medicine to a sick boy.
George realizes Gower gave him the wrong medicine—a poi-
son, in fact. He returns to the pharmacy, bad stuff undelivered,
and happens upon an opened telegram conveying tragic news:
Gower's son has just died.

The pharmacist is burning with the acid agony of fresh grief.
And he's drunk. Blurrily furious that the meds were not deliv-
ered, Gower lunges at George, boxing his ears, drawing blood,
staggering through sobs and tremors. "Don't you know that boy's
sick?" he croaks.

Little George Bailey's response is amazing. He's under violent assault, but he doesn't strike back. Instead he cries, "Mr. Gower, you don't know what you're doing. You put something wrong in those capsules. I know why you hit me. You got the telegram and you're upset. You put something bad in those capsules. It wasn't your fault, Mr. Gower!"

Gower discovers George is telling the truth, falls to his knees, and embraces him in alcohol-soaked gratitude. There will be no further violence that morning, only understanding—all due to George's clear-eyed choice to comfort an old man enduring the worst day of his life.

Powerful stuff, this executive function.

The Executive Function Trinity

As stated before, most scientists concur that EF includes a trio of interactive elements[18] (see Figure 1.1).

Response inhibition (also called effortful control, self-control, emotional self-regulation, and impulse control) involves ignoring a compelling natural tendency in favor of another behavioral option. Resisting sensory temptations (e.g., adultery, ice cream sundaes, designer shoes) or not striking back at someone who is threatening (Mr. Gower) are examples. The core behavior involves controlling what we pay attention to, ignoring certain stimuli, and attending to others.

The second element, *cognitive flexibility,* allows individuals to adapt to changing circumstances with the litheness of a Cirque du Soleil acrobat. It includes the ability to see objective problems (or subjective people) from multiple perspectives, switch perspectives, and notice when perspectives switch. George didn't strike back at Mr. Gower because, having seen the telegram, he was able to assess the situation from the viewpoint of the grieving pharmacist. Mr. Gower exhibited perspective switching, too,

Defining Executive Function

Figure 1.1

The exact definition of executive function is controversial, but most researchers agree it has three core elements.

1  **Response inhibition** (also called self-regulation, impulse control, self-control) involves saying no to certain impulses, yes to others. The key behaviors include deciding what input we pay attention to and how we respond to it.

2  **Cognitive flexibility** is the ability to adapt to changing circumstances in a tractable manner. This includes perspective switching—the ability to see objective problems (or subjective people) from multiple perspectives or points of view.

3  **Working memory** (formerly known as "short-term memory") comprises a series of cognitive buffers that temporarily store information. Different buffers hold different types of inputs (visual vs. auditory, for example).

For more information, see Adele Diamond, "Executive Functions," *Annual Review of Psychology* 64 (2013): 135–68.

changing his behavior when he realized George had not endangered the sick boy's life but saved it.

The third component is *working memory,* a retrieval system that is sometimes called short-term memory. Researcher Alan Baddeley (who looks unnervingly like Henry Travers, the actor who played angel Clarence Odbody in *It's a Wonderful Life*) showed that working memory is where information is stored temporarily in the pursuit of a goal.[19] It is made up of a series of buffers, each assigned to store different things. One buffer, termed the phonological loop, holds verbal information. Another, called the visuospatial sketch pad, transiently holds images and other spatial inputs. There's even a buffer designed to keep track of the others named the central executive. A number of years ago, Baddeley added a final category, the episodic buffer, which holds information couched in the form of stories.

Of Darwin and Genetics

Neural substrates underwrite these three behaviors with the thoroughness of a stress-tested bank. Like all biological tissues, these nerves were forged in the iron furnaces of evolution. Researchers are beginning to understand the selective pressures—the Darwinian hammers and anvils—that shaped the nerves during humanity's collective Serengeti sojourn. They took form not because humans were so strong, but because we were so weak.

I know that sounds oxymoronic. In our fragile, naked, not-very-hairy physical bodies lies little hint of any internal power that could crown us Earth's apex predator. Yet that's what humans became. If we relied purely on corporeal evolution, we might have had to wait 24 million generations to become big and strong and essentially invulnerable, like elephants (who actually did have to wait 24 million generations).[20] The anthropological record shows we *didn't* wait those gazillion years to become Earth's most dangerous badasses, and yet here we are, indisputably in charge. What in the world happened?

Enter executive function, taking center stage like a diva.

It's a strange kind of prima donna. Rather than causing us to be consistently narcissistic, executive function allows us to be steadily cooperative. With brains capable of not only *understanding* one another's psychological interiors but also *tolerating* one another's psychological interiors, we learned to coordinate our behaviors. From there, humans began cooperating to pursue common goals, like systematizing our hunts and dividing our labors.

We needed not big strong bodies to do this, but big strong brains—and developing those allowed humans to spend a lot less time in the evolutionary gym. Executive function guided this process. It lubricated our social interactions so that coordination often defeated confrontation. Then it defeated every other species. Those ancestors who excelled in EF lived long enough to further excel by passing on their genes.

This statement suggests that proficiency in EF is as heritable as a family fortune. Here's the shocker: it is. The title of the research paper by the team that discovered this fact says it all: "Individual Differences in Executive Functions Are Almost Entirely Genetic in Origin." According to these researchers, executive function has the highest heritability for a complex behavioral suite ever recorded, with the individual variance weighing in at a whopping 99 percent.[21]

Yep, the ability George Bailey has to understand Mr. Gower lies somewhere in George's genes. And in ours, too. Genetics aren't the whole story, of course. There's that nature/nurture stuff to contend with (data exist demonstrating that it's not only willpower that influences what we do with marshmallows at age 4, for example; the perceived reliability of the reward is a factor, too).[22] But without invoking the double helix of DNA at some point, the Darwinian picture is woefully incomplete.

Hunting Like a Little Girl

The image on the cover of *National Geographic Traveler* magazine captures a smiling 13-year-old girl straddling a wind-carved Mongolian mountaintop; on her arm is a flapping eagle that is literally as big as she is. Her name is Aisholpan Nurgaiv, and she is the youngest Eagle Hunter—make that Eagle *Huntress*—in the world.[23]

There are two remarkable things about Aisholpan. First, she is blessed with a spine made of titanium. Girls in Mongolian culture aren't supposed to hunt with eagles; it's a fully ritualized falconry-meets-grocery-shopping activity with a big cultural sign on its neck that reads "males only." Yet her determination to learn was as unmoving as the Altai mountains of her homeland. Facing gale-force winds of social rejection, Aisholpan trained relentlessly in the unforgiving winters of Western Mongolia (the grown men of the film crew who were following her around could barely keep up). Even when she became successful, the male elders in her community made excuses to explain away her accomplishments, saying she had a great bird or a great coach, or she was just seeking publicity.

The second remarkable thing about Aisholpan is the talented organ topping that metal spine. She is whip-smart and ambitious. She's learned Turkish and English. She snagged a scholarship to a school in Mongolia and wants to be a surgeon. The film eventually made about her, *The Eagle Huntress*, became wildly successful, and some of its proceeds will be used to develop Aisholpan's brain further by funding her pursuit of higher education.

It's no coincidence that extraordinary self-control and extraordinary intellectual accomplishment are joined at the hip. Put simply, this combo gives kids the intellectual talons necessary to tear into hard problems. The twin peaks of response inhibition and academic achievement predict success in virtually every country where such behaviors have been studied. That Aisholpan Nurgaiv is an exemplar of a fascinating area of brain science is probably not something the camera crews would have ever expected. And yet she is.

Self-Control

Aisholpan's determined self-control is as obvious as the steely grin on the Eagle Huntress's face. There are several definitions for self-control, and the responsibility and determination that fortifies Aisholpan's character easily fit most of them. Scientists Roy Baumeister and his colleagues have even invented psychometric tests to measure the behavior. These tests, now very much the gold standard used to measure this aspect of executive function, have been found to be both reliable and valid.[24]

Not only that, these tests are prophetic. Put simply, executive function acts as a scientific Nostradamus. It can actually predict how kids will turn out as students, and then go on to predict how they will turn out as adults. Whether you examine cross-sectional data, longitudinal data, associative studies, or direct interventions, high scores on executive function measures predict future success at teenagers and adults. *And it's practically the only thing that does.*

Here's how Baumeister and Tierney put it:

> When researchers compared students' grades with nearly three dozen personality traits, self-control turned out to be the *only* trait that predicted a college student's grade-point average better than chance. Self-control also proved to be a better predictor of college grades than the student's IQ or SAT score.[25] (emphasis in original)

The fact that executive function separates rock star from rock bottom is the primary reason teachers (and parents, too) should know about EF and focus on it when interacting with the adolescents in their charge.

Weed-Whacking

I realize that linking executive function and academic (and future) success so strongly is provocative. There are researchers who are skeptical of the connection. I recall one review article that went so far as to bluntly dismiss the assertion that EF boosts student outcomes in reading and math, stating: "No compelling evidence that a causal association between the two exists."[26] Yet another paper claims just the opposite and does so decisively, as you can discern from its title: "Executive Function Predicts Reading, Mathematics and Theory of Mind During the Elementary Years."[27]

What can we do with this conflict? I'll have more to say about the tenuous relationship between correlation and causation in a little bit. Suffice it to say, the preponderance of data appear to cluster around executive function like adoring fans at a book signing.

Here's the bottom line: as a teacher, you want your classroom populated with as many Aisholpans as you can find. They get along better with teachers and are popular with peers. They achieve better academic outcomes in part because they have better study habits. They have terrific attendance records. They start their homework earlier, spend more quality time with it, and are less seduced by electronic screens, the great digital temptress of the West.

The data are becoming granular enough that we can predict which cognitive gadgets relate to which specific classroom skill. Flexibility scores all by themselves predict success in mathematics. We also know that when all three pistons of executive function—response inhibition, cognitive flexibility, and working memory—are firing at the same time, reading comprehension goes up. No wonder kids with strong EF scores do better after they traverse the crevasses of puberty and find their way to college.

Of course, these warm-and-fuzzy data describe kids with high executive function, which is only one side of the story. What about those with low EF? Do their scores also predict their future—one that's perhaps not as warm and fuzzy?

The answer is depressing, with the most striking results coming from the behavioral work. Kids with low self-control scores are more likely to be expelled from *preschool* (it starts that early).[28] They often percolate through their elementary years with anger management issues (tantrums) and become more socially aggressive with age.[29] To no one's surprise, their grades in primary school stink. By adolescence, these kids are at greater risk for every behavior we'd rather they say no to.[30] They're more likely to engage in unprotected sex, abuse drugs, and enter the juvenile system.[31] And their grades still stink.

Other Cultures

Amid these darkening data, I would like to light a candle.

First, let me say that I believe deeply in the incandescent power of world cultures interacting with one other, which is something I see in my profession and across the country every day. The research groups around our universities generally look more like the United Nations than they do many parts of the United States. There's a lot of hope in this diversity, especially in the passive transfer of behavior (including executive function; more about this transference later).

Nonetheless, I admit becoming as hot as a Szechuan peppercorn when I picked up the 2011 best-seller *Battle Hymn of the Tiger Mother* by Amy Chua, where I read about behaviors that seemed more a blowtorch than a hope-inspiring candle of cultural amalgamation.[32] Chua allowed her two daughters no playdates. No boyfriends, either. They studied six hours a day and were drilled with music lessons using a method so draconian it was detailed in the Wikipedia entry for the book. One adolescent daughter was told that if a complex piano piece wasn't mastered in 24 hours, her mother would dismember her dollhouse, then donate the pieces, one at a time, to the Salvation Army. Tiger Mom didn't let her take a break—not for dinner, not for the toilet, not for a drink of water—until she nailed the piece. Which eventually she did.[33]

After finishing the book, I was left with several candle-lighting impressions. First, it was clear to me that Chua hadn't written a parenting book; she'd written a memoir, and much of it, as she says, is distilled self-parody. Second, Chua's children became wildly successful, graduating from the most prestigious universities in the world. "We are a close family," the piano-playing daughter said in an interview. "Even when there was a lot of screaming, that was work. When it was over, that was family time and we'd go upstairs and watch movies together."[34]

Third, there was something vaguely appealing to me about the Tiger Mother's old-fashioned discipline. Some of her parenting choices struck me as bordering on child abuse, and, as a brain development scientist, I can hardly recommend her style. Yet Chua was a regular visitor to an important sector in the land of executive function. As I will address later in the book, researchers investigating parenting phenomena have discovered some extraordinary things about a behavioral style called *authoritative parenting.* It turns out that some of Chua's technique sailed on the trade winds of good sense.

All Roads Lead to China

Chua's book brings into consideration another aspect relating to executive function skills in children and adolescents: the important-as-oxygen cultural issues. She acquired her belief in discipline from her parents, immigrants from China, and was regularly exposed to people whose social currency had a tradition of strong academic achievement. What would we find if we measured effortful control in students from countries with such strong, successful traditions?

That work has been done, and the results won't surprise you. First, the effortful control scores of kids in Asian countries that are broadly considered to be strongly focused on academics are stratospheric. Joining them at altitude are their academic scores; the top achievers on the international PISA assessments include Shanghai, Hong Kong, Singapore, Japan, and South Korea.[35]

What about the good old USA? Years ago, researcher Larry Steinberg tested impulse control in subjects across the Chinese educational food chain (ages 10–30), comparing them to age-matched controls in the United States. Amazingly, he found no real differences between the results put up by 4th graders (10-year-olds) in the two countries.

Unfortunately, the good news didn't stay good. Like a slow-moving earthquake, a fissure soon created a gap between the two cultures. By age 14, Chinese kids scored 20 percent higher than their U.S. counterparts; by age 18, it was 45 percent higher. The score differential peaked at age 20, at 50 percent.[36] Does that sound familiar? You might recall the Evel Knievel story that started this chapter. U.S. student scores are competitive with the rest of the world up until 4th grade—then they fall off a cliff.

Another instance of cultural influence on executive function can be found in our country's immigrant population. A broad mixture of families, many from high-scoring cultures, immigrate to the United States and enroll their children in American schools. Does transplantation affect their kids' academic performance? Do behavioral differences persist?

The answer, simply put, is that they carry their good stuff with them. Many immigrant kids thrive here—academically, behaviorally, and socially. This is true even in the face of the cultural headwinds immigrants naturally experience when trying to integrate into a new place. The phenomenon is so widespread, and so counterintuitive, it's been given its own name: the immigrant paradox.[37]

Correlation Is Not Causation

As mentioned, not everybody buys this executive function cheerleading, and I'd like to talk about why.

Did you know that the annual number of Americans who died because they became entangled by their bedsheets correlates beautifully with the annual total revenue generated by U.S. skiing facilities? Measured between the years 2000 and 2009, the two graphs rise and fall together like twin snakes doing a synchronized swimming routine. Believe it or not, this fact, taken from the terrific website Spurious Correlations, is relevant to our purposes. Here are a few more curious but relevant facts to ponder. The marriage rate in North Carolina correlates (with similar serpentine elegance) with the state's number of legal executions, whereas the marriage rate in Alabama correlates with the number of people electrocuted by power lines.[38]

Why bring up such nonsense? Because a lot of the previously described behavioral data, as promising as they seem, remain plagued by correlational disease, which usually has a rocky relationship with causality. This is true with any study of descriptive research. Correlation is not causation, as marriages in the southern United States do not really affect the rate of particular forms of violent death—at least, we hope they don't.

Correlational data isn't useless math, of course. Demonstrations of its power come from observing student EF scores and future adult outcomes. You just have to be able to tolerate the strong flavor of complex statistics. And you must follow "kids" for decades, in a canonical longitudinal study. Such studies are both hard and expensive to do. Yet real findings have emerged, including an adult version of the same high-score-good/low-score-bad story. (And to be fair, terrific "intervention" studies have also been done, which we'll discuss later.) The bottom line is that the predictive relationship between executive function and future outcome remains strong, even as the subjects become AARP-eligible.

Oversimplification

As I've emphasized, the correlations between strong executive function and positive long-term outcomes last well into adulthood. Physical appearance was an early, startling finding, especially when subjects were asked to step on their bathroom scales. Students with high EF had lower body mass indices (BMI) as adults, and they kept the weight off in middle age. Their rates of substance abuse, including alcohol, were lower, too. They even had healthier teeth.

High scorers on measures of EF were more empathetic, had more friends, and were less likely to experience psychiatric disorders (especially anxiety and depression). They didn't get angry very often, and they were less prone to divorce. Such stability was rewarded in the workforce with the ultimate laurel: they earned higher salaries.

The story for low self-regulators was contrastingly depressing. Subjects were more likely to be fat, to abuse alcohol, and to divorce. They got angrier more often, were more prone to domestic violence, and were more likely to be incarcerated— and not at a trivial rate. Greater than 40 percent of the kids with the lowest scores were already scarlet-lettered with a criminal conviction by age 32. (In contrast, only 12 percent of control subjects had convictions by that age.)[39]

It's easy to want to applaud these findings, but easy to roll your eyes at them, too. They probably deserve neither reaction, though, especially concerning teenagers and their GPAs. Researchers offer many reasons to explain poor academic performance in teens. Some fault parents for not providing challenging learning environments at home. Others fault teachers for not providing the same at school. Some believe teens are bored and lose interest. Others believe boredom is just another word for overindulged laziness. Racial bias exists in the way tests are constructed; similar bias persists in the way school districts are structured.

Cultural issues are messy as well. The United States deals with unique social challenges, from a searing racial history to the "usual suspects" of low socioeconomic status (poverty, depression, and family fracture come to mind). We're also the richest country the world has ever seen, making our challenges unlike those of any other nation on Earth. This makes cross-cultural comparisons difficult.

That's the beauty of the executive function data that have been collected. The cited research has addressed most of these confounders, some in meticulous detail. I'm not shy about keeping complexity in mind—after all, I'm a brain scientist. Yet when the statistical dust settles, what's left in these data is a clearly understandable problem with a potentially powerful bromide. And executive function research has happily blessed us with one of the valuable traits in all of science: the power of prediction.

Our challenge—which is by no means small—is to understand the teenage brain. Our elixir is the application of brain science. Since students fall off the academic cliff around puberty, understanding what happens under the hood of a typically developing adolescent brain is extremely valuable knowledge that will give us better insight about what happens when things go wrong.

Understanding the problems may even show us the way to fix them—or at least get us started on constructing the bridge we need to span the canyon.

PART II

WHY RATIONAL TEENS MAKE RASH CHOICES

It's time for a closer examination of how the teen brain looks and how the teen brain grows—to describe the neurobiology behind executive function, and then see how this understanding applies to learning. We'll consider EF's adult form and delve into how it got there, and we'll use a neurological lens to scrutinize the contradictory aspects of adolescent behavior, from the heart warming to the stupid.

Our discussion starts in New York City, with a description of one of the most controversial shows that MTV ever broadcast. . . .

2

BRAIN STRUCTURE

The TV program was called *Jackass*. And boy, did the show deserve that title.

For those not familiar with it, MTV's *Jackass* involved a group of guys doing risky, occasionally life-threatening stunts, all live for the camera. There were many variations, from taking a ride in a limo filled with bees to creating the legendary "poo-cano" (don't ask). Teenagers loved the show, probably for the same reasons teenagers love unprotected sex and binge drinking.

Adolescents worldwide attempted to reproduce the stunts they watched. They set themselves on fire, leapt out of buildings, and jumped over moving objects. Some died, many more were injured, and a few became parties to lawsuits (the litigants were usually parents).[1] These actions seemed to confirm a pervasive stereotype: teenagers can do really stupid stuff. They make poor, impulsive decisions. They don't understand the consequences of their behaviors. They become peer-needy thrill seekers. Sounds like their executive function warriors went missing in action.

Statistics seem to bear this assessment out. Teenagers *do* engage in risky behaviors. They take more risks than they did as younger children, and take more risks than they will as adults. For evidence, look no further than your insurance bill. Automobile insurance premiums are higher for teenagers than for any other group, and highest for teenage boys. That's because motor vehicle accidents are the leading cause of death in this age group, responsible for half of all teen fatalities. The second and third biggest causes of teen death—homicide and suicide, respectively—are no less alarming or tragic. Researcher BJ Casey puts the risk this way: "The bad news is that during this time, relative to childhood, [a teen's] chances of dying from putting themselves in harm's way will increase by 200 percent."[2]

That's Not the Whole Story

Given these data, you might feel like putting the teens you care about into a witness protection program until they reach adulthood, just for their own safety. There's no question that there are lots of examples of scary teenage activity, but it's important to understand that the age group is not a monolithic entity following a single behavioral path. Research shows that adolescents don't *always* choose to be stupid. They *are* capable of rational decisions. Consider this true story of a nonagenarian, a flooded house in southeast Texas, and three alert teens.

Sallie Cole, a 93-year-old grandmother, knew she was in trouble. The rains were coming down in biblical torrents in Kountz, Texas. The water was rising and would soon flood her home. As she lived alone and could only get around using a walker, the situation was shaping up to become a life-threatening one.

Three local teenagers, the medal-worthy heroes of this story, deduced the danger that Sallie faced. Forming a rescue party, they swam to Sallie's front door and then created a human sedan chair: they locked arms and carried her to safety in style! Once she was in a safe place, they swam back to the house and retrieved her walker.

A grateful Sallie asked if she could offer them payment. They said no. Instead, they left her with their phone numbers, encouraging her to call if flood waters ever threatened again (nearly a sure bet in southeast Texas). They even volunteered to return to handle clean up once the water subsided. "If you need any yardwork or anything, we'll be happy to help you," one said. The trio then spent the rest of the day assisting other people in similar situations.[3]

This may just be a single example, but it makes a larger point: teens aren't always jackasses. They are fully capable of making rational, even heroic, choices.

Why, then, don't they make them more often? The answer has powerful implications for education, and we'll spend the next two chapters exploring it. I want to start with some background brain facts, though, before embarking on the neurologically based explanations. That way, if it's been a while since you took a basic biology class, you'll be better prepared to understand how executive function develops in teens and why that development takes place so unevenly. Along the way, we will discover the difference between *Jackass* teens and Sallie-rescuing teens—as well as a thing or two about ourselves.

State of Mind

Let's start our discussion about basic brain biology with a question: if you could magically hold your own adult brain in your own adult hands, what would you think? (Besides, perhaps, wondering how you could see anything at all.)

Most probably, you'd be completely surprised—or maybe grossed out—not by its color (pinkish white, mostly from blood), and perhaps not by its shape (it looks like a big walnut). You'd probably react most strongly to its squishiness. For all its hardwired complexity, the brain is much softer than almost any meat you're likely to encounter in, say, a supermarket. If you continue to hold it for even a few seconds, the brain will start to deform around your fingers, like it's melting.[4] It's not melting, of course. But its startling physical vulnerability will hardly make you think you are beholding the most complex computing device the world has ever known.

And yet you are. Your brain is a thinking machine, comfortably floating in a salty hot tub set to a balmy 98.6 degrees Fahrenheit. It's protected by a biological Fort Knox, with tough tissues surrounded by a rock-hard skull. These layers of protection guard the 86 billion nerve cells crammed into two lopsided hemispheres roughly the size of your two fists, with about 186 million more brain cells on the left side than on the right. And these cells, only about 10 percent of which are really neurons, form more than 60 trillion chatty connections with one another (the other 90 percent are termed *glial* cells, which, for no good reason, means "glue"). Some neurons have 1,000 connections to other nerve cells, which seems like a lot until you compare them to others, like the ones involved in motor functions, which can have more than 100,000.

Like teenagers in high school, your brain cells and accompanying tissues form extremely active social networks. They also gobble up lots of power. Though your brain is only 2 percent of your body weight, it demands 20 percent of all your energy. It's got a finicky sweet tooth, too, extracting energy only from sugars and leaving fats alone. Cut off the blood supply, which provides both sweets and waste disposal services, and you're about 10 seconds from loss of consciousness, 2 minutes away from loss of reflex, and 6 minutes away from loss of life.[5]

How can we describe an organ whose complexity rivals that of the U.S. tax code? One way to simplify things is to consider the human brain like a state or province, complete with cities, highways, and geographic features. Many of the original neuroanatomists seized on this analogy, using civic words to name much of what they identified. There's a region called the *pons,* Latin for "bridge" (its discoverer said it reminded him of one). There's the *fornix,* meaning "arch," so named for the same reason. There's a region called the *cerebral aqueduct,* like the Roman stone equivalent; *cisterns,* meaning "reservoirs"; and *tectum,* meaning "roof."

Geographic features also abound in this heady metaphor. Your brain has *gyri* (ridges), *sulci* (valleys), an *insula* (island), and a *hilum,* which literally means "unimportant thing" (they're critical, actually, and you have many of them). There's a group of tissue collectively termed the *limbic system,* which means "border," based on the idea it looks like the boundary between two neural "counties," the brain stem and the cerebral structures blossoming above it.[6]

Some areas of the brain are somewhat self-contained regions charged with doling out specific functions; these can be thought of as "cities." The oldest city is in the center of your brain, sometimes referred to as the "lizard brain" because it functions in lizards the same way it functions in us (looks like a lizard's brain, too). The newest city (in evolutionary terms) is the region just behind your forehead, the *prefrontal cortex.* You might call this region the human brain, because no other creature has it. Most of the functions that define our species, including critical aspects of executive function, originate here. Figure 2.1 presents a diagram of these areas' locations.

The quaint anatomical terms used for brain components reflect the thinking of the times when they were first identified (generally the late 19th century) more than modern neurological understanding. Some of the biggest changes in our knowledge concern the neural connections between regions, the "highways" linking our metaphorical cities. Many of the brain's most powerful functions occur along these connections, and there are many to choose from. There are large interstate freeways, smaller state highways, narrow neurological boulevards, and tiny cellular alleys. The two highways we'll spend the most time discussing connect the prefrontal cortex with those lizardlike structures near the center of your brain. Interestingly, no two highway systems are exactly the same in any two brains, even those of identical twins. That means that every brain is hooked up differently from every other brain, which has enormous implications for human behavior—especially when we talk about executive function.

The Brains Behind Executive Function

Figure 2.1

Executive function involves reciprocating electrical communications between large areas of the brain, two of which are shown below.

Limbic Structures
Responsible for many functions, including the generation of emotional responses, creating and processing memories, and originating "basic" appetites, such as the desire for food and sex.

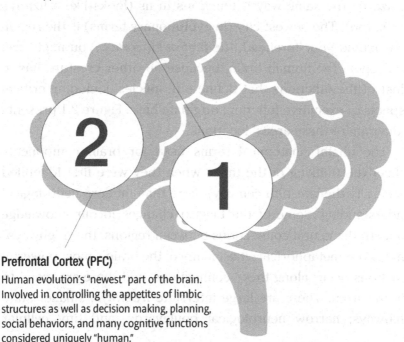

Prefrontal Cortex (PFC)
Human evolution's "newest" part of the brain. Involved in controlling the appetites of limbic structures as well as decision making, planning, social behaviors, and many cognitive functions considered uniquely "human."

We'll get to that in moment. Right now, we're going to take a trip to Disney World!

Hidden Structures

Tucked inside a gigantic 18-story geodesic dome, Spaceship Earth is the first attraction you see on entering Walt Disney World's extraordinary Epcot.

The ride is easily my favorite Disney experience. You're seated in a car on a slow-moving conveyor belt, embarking on a stately ride through the history of human communication. Spiraling up the dome's interior, you begin with cave drawings and end with Apple Computers. I've been on the ride dozens of times.

On one of those occasions, an annoying malfunction occurred, literally halting the cars in their tracks in the middle of the journey. Mine was parked next to a burning aqueduct scene. Its unpleasant smell remained in my nostrils for hours afterward, but I did get a chance to examine the dome's interior structure. What I saw was lots of cleverly hidden scaffolding, trusses, metal struts, and reinforcing bars, all designed to support the snaking tracks that carried the cars as they ascended 180 feet through the structure. I have since decided that Spaceship Earth is an ideal illustration of the human brain's structural interior.

As mentioned, you can divide brain cells into two overarching types, glial cells and neurons. Glial cells, which make up 90 percent of the organ's cellular population, are like Spaceship Earth's interior scaffolding. Neurons, which make up the other 10 percent, are like the tracks that spiral through it.

For years, scientists thought glial cells were involved only in unintelligent structural support, providing the cellular corner braces, floor joists, and load-bearing walls for the "thinking parts" of the human brain. Now we know that while they do perform these functions, that's just their day job. Glia are also nursemaids, sanitation engineers, morticians, and signal processors, playing a role in the care and feeding of neurons, removing their ever-present molecular garbage, adding to brain health by getting rid of dead cells, and assisting with electrical communications throughout the brain.[7]

Neurons, however, usually get all the media attention. The typical brain contains 86 billion neurons in a bewildering number of shapes and sizes, though they do have some common structural elements, highlighted in Figure 2.2.

Basic Neural Anatomy

Figure 2.2

Though neurons come in a wide variety of shapes and sizes, they share basic structures, highlighted in the simplified diagram below.

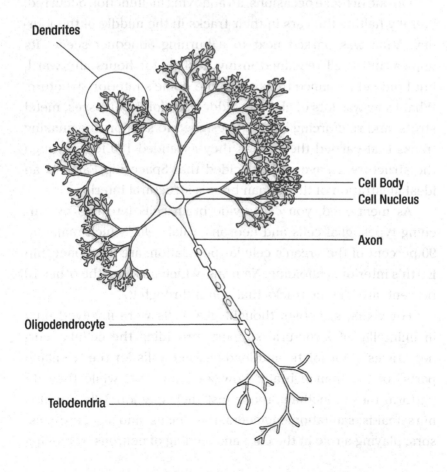

Dendrites

Cell Body
Cell Nucleus

Axon

Oligodendrocyte

Telodendria

One easy way to visualize these elements is to stretch out your arm and inspect it, from fingers to elbow. When you do, you are looking at the general shape of a neuron. Like your forearm, one end of a neuron has lots of branchlike "fingers" called *dendrites*. The "hand" to which the dendrites connect is the *cell body,* which contains the nucleus of the cell. The nucleus possesses the neuron's genetic instructions, complete with cellular command-and-control.

The "arm" connecting the cell body to the neural elbow is the *axon.* Unlike your flexor-strung appendage, the axon is quite slender and can be long. The longest human axon is the dorsal nerve root ganglia (DNRG), which runs from the base of your spinal column to your big toe, about 3 feet in length. The world-record length for *any* axon belongs to the blue whale's DNRG, however, at about 75 feet.

Our arm analogy starts breaking down when we consider the neuronal "elbow," because this end of the cell doesn't look anything like an elbow. It's composed of tiny fingers called *telodendria,* which are similar to dendrites though smaller in number. Telodendria are chock-full of chemicals termed *neurotransmitters,* which are critical to the communication abilities of the brain.

These abilities are as electrical as Las Vegas. The neurons that contain the brain's bustling energy are hooked up in a linear, branching fashion, comprising the circuits necessary to pass along that electrical information. The signal flows from the dendrites (fingers) down through the axon (arm) to the telodendria (elbow)—where they immediately encounter a problem. There's a gap, a space that must be crossed, between the elbow of one neuron and the fingertip of another. One of the most interesting aspects of the connected world of neural wiring is that it's not physically connected at all.

This tiny gulf is called a synapse, meaning "joins together," though it should really be called "joins apart." Neurons jump this

space using neurotransmitters, the ones stuffed into the telodendria. Neurotransmitters act like molecular couriers. When neuron A becomes electrically excited, it spits those couriers into
the space. The molecules make the short commute, binding to
receptor molecules on adjacent neuron B. Very quickly, neuron
B reacts, evidence that information has successfully traversed
the synapse. Sometimes it reacts by getting excited. Sometimes
it reacts by shutting down.[8]

All of this, of course, is an enormous oversimplification. For
deeper understanding, some other ingredients must be added to
the mix.

Wire Cutters

Everyone who's ever watched an action movie knows the
scenario: there's a bomb, it's attached to a timer, and that
timer is counting down the seconds until massive, maybe even
world-ending, destruction. To save the day, the doughty protagonist tears open the fearsome weapon's outer casing to reveal
a mass of colored wires (they're always colored wires). He (it's
always a he) pauses, wire cutters in hand. If he clips the right
wire, he defuses the bomb. *But which wire is the right wire?*

You'll find a variation of this trope in the final scenes of *The
Abyss.* The familiar clichés are dutifully present: the action hero
is male, the bomb is atomic, and he must save the world by
cutting a specific color of wire. This time, though, our hero is
a gazillion feet underwater, with only a sickly yellow glow stick
for light. Unfortunately, that glow stick renders all the wires the
same color, which is a problem because one's black-and-white,
the other yellow-and-blue. Fortunately, the film is directed by
James Cameron, not Ingmar Bergman; the hero guesses right,
and we all live to watch another movie.

Why are those wires colored, anyway? We just discussed
what a standard-issue neuron looks like, but I omitted something
crucial: the outer covering many neurons have around their

axons. This coating is important to our discussion of executive function. To describe it, we need to talk a little bit about electricity and a lot about the reason wires are pigmented.

Electrical wires are usually made of copper, so what's with all the black and white and yellow and blue? These multicolored coatings around the copper serve two purposes: (1) to help designate specific circuits, and (2) to provide electrical insulation. Obviously, being able to identify wires by color is beneficial, but why do wires need insulation in the first place?

Insulation Solutions

Wires are insulated for the same reason you buy winter coats. If it's cold outside, you wear a coat to keep your vital 98.6 degrees inside your body, recycling its warmth to provide the heat you won't get from the great outdoors. Similarly, if you don't slap a coat on the wire, the current will dissipate from the copper into the great outdoors, and the electricity will have a hard time performing any useful function.

Neurons face the same problem. Like their copper colleagues, without insulation, their circuits won't work well. Neurons have solved this problem in an interesting way. To both visualize and describe how it works, I'd like to bring back my forearm-as-neuron analogy.

Go ahead and stick your arm out again, but this time wrap a towel around your arm several times. That's an awkward but adequate visualization of how neurons insulate themselves. They possess a type of hand towel, a living cell that wraps around their axons like the cloth around your arm. Brain scientists call this cell an *oligodendrocyte,* a type of glial cell. It performs similar insulating functions, allowing the wrapped-up neuron to conduct electricity efficiently.

The insulating secret sauce inside oligodendrocytes is a biochemical called myelin, a substance made of the same stuff you find in a Snickers bar—fats, salts, and proteins. Myelin is also colored, if you consider white a color. Because myelin appears grayish-white under the microscope, we term neurons wrapped by oligodendrocytes "white matter."

Myelin's insulating properties help neurons deliver signals with as much speed as a Japanese bullet train—a blistering 100 meters per second. In neurons without myelin, the signal travels through neurological molasses, poking along at 1 meter per second. Myelin's critical function is pointed out by the fact that its erosion results in a devastating disease: the onset of multiple sclerosis.[9]

Interestingly, you aren't born with all the myelin you need in your brain. This means you will need to finish brain development outside the womb. It's an extremely slow process, however: white matter volume doesn't peak until you get your first AARP letter, about 50 years after birth.[10]

By the way, the cell body (the "hand" in our arm analogy) isn't insulated with myelin, so it's not white. But it still has a color under the microscope, and that color is gray. Unwrapped areas (dendrites, cell bodies, even a few axons) are collectively called "gray matter." We suddenly have the origins of two neuroanatomical words you've probably heard before: white matter and gray matter. Both are significant when it comes to discussing executive function and teen brain development.

Mark Twain and Executive Function

Here's my favorite Mark Twain quote, which has surprising relevance to our modern understanding of EF and neurons:

> When I was a boy of 14, my father was so ignorant I could hardly stand to have the old man around. But when I got to be 21, I was astonished at how much the old man had learned in seven years.

The quote's meaningful to me not for its breezy irony, but for its not-so-breezy context. These words are not autobiographical.

Twain's father died when Twain was a boy of 11. Young Samuel L. Clemens left school the next year and went on to receive much of his subsequent education from the University of Public Libraries, where he learned a lot about life—perhaps even about how other boys react to living fathers.

I also like the quote for its rueful surrender to the power of experience. Time, it turns out, is the ripening agent of executive function, a fact that translates into actual brain science. Much of the brain's physical architecture is shaped by experience through time. We won't understand how adult EF works until we understand how its cellular fields of gray and white are affected by this shaping, which requires describing two more concepts.

Concept #1: Deep Specialization

Brain function is remarkably specialized. Consider the regions responsible for the concept of "animals." You process the word "giraffe" in regions different from where you process the giraffe's actual image. If a stroke destroys neural connections between the two, you might be able to write the word "giraffe," and even describe one physically, yet you'd be unable to recognize its picture.

Other regions are equally finicky. Some will only respond to straight lines tilted at 45 degrees, no giraffe in sight. Other regions process only 30-degree-tilted lines, not 45-degree ones. One area, the *fusiform gyrus,* doesn't do lines at all. It's specialized for faces, complete with eyes and mouths, and not legs and ski masks. Still other regions process feelings—love, disgust, fear—completely separate from giraffes, tilted lines, and faces.

These regions are as connected to each other as a pyramid scheme, helping us interpret the experiences of life. If you observe a grasshopper leg tilted at 45 degrees, it's because neurons that recognize the insect start electrically chatting away with neurons responsible for 45-degree-line processing. The combination helps produce the perception.

Emotions are integrated into these combinations, too. Suppose Mark Twain's dad had lived. If Mr. Clemens walked in the room, Samuel's 14-year-old brain would recognize him instantly, perhaps with disgust, as his face-processor dialed up his disgust processor and the two started communicating like texting teenagers. Enough experience might weld the connections together. What those patterns look like depends on the type of experience being, well, experienced.[11]

Concept #2: Deep Connections

The neurological wiring diagram bringing these functions together has been unimaginatively christened the *connectome*. With at least 100 trillion synapses, the connectome is the most complex schematic ever discovered. Its complexity is made worse because much of it is plastic, moving and shifting with the flexibility of a Hogwarts staircase.

Not every region is adaptable, however. Some connections come hardwired at birth, supervising life's basic "housekeeping" functions. Infants are illustrative. Though controlled by connecting neurons, nobody teaches babies' brains how to breathe or keep their hearts beating. These schematics are experience-*independent*.

Other connectome parts are completely free-range, as flexible as ballet dancers, available to learn virtually anything experience throws at them. Almost everything instructors explain at school (and parents explain at home) is processed in these lithe regions of the connectome. In other words, parts of the brain are hardwired not to be hardwired at all; they are experience-*dependent*.

Some regions are simultaneously hardwired and free-range. Language is a great example. All babies are born with the ability to speak a language (that's hardwired), but no baby is born with the specific ability to speak Mandarin (that's free-range). The visual system is another example. Brains actually require photic experience—meaning they need to see external light—to wire properly. This wiring is experience-*expectant.*

Some members of this category possess genetic time bombs embedded in their nuclear DNA. These "bombs," which are really executable neurological programs, won't go off until a certain amount of time has passed. This can be months, or even years. Puberty's an excellent example. All hormones and supervising reproductive instructions are programmed into babies at birth, but years will pass before the obnoxious door slamming, eye rolling, moodiness, and other classic manifestations of adolescent drama start. We call such malware "developmental programs."[12]

Of Gladiators and Brains

I love chariot races in period-piece movies the way some people love chocolate. Or ripped abs. These scenes also provide another convenient way to describe the neurobiology of executive function, the subject to which we now turn.

My first exposure to a chariot race—William Wyler's classic 1959 *Ben-Hur*—almost spoiled me for the rest. The second was less impressive and came in the early scenes of the animated *The Prince of Egypt.* The third chariot race, another step down (but still awesome, of course), was in the technically challenged *Gladiator.* All of the chariots in these races have the same three elements: drivers, horses, and the connecting reins allowing the drivers to control the horses (except for *Gladiator,* where the chariot has a 21st-century gas cylinder attached to its underside, the better to flip it over during a crash; you can see this cylinder easily when the set's dust settles over the ancient hippodrome).[13] The basic design elements of these vehicles (sans gas cylinder) make a great metaphor for describing the neurobiology of mature executive function: the driver is the prefrontal cortex (PFC), the horses are the "lizard brain," and the reins are the neurological connections between the two.

The Charioteer

The PFC lies directly behind your forehead and is evolution's most recent addition to our cognitive pantheon. It's as huge as Thebes, taking up almost a third of the cerebral footprint and by several measures the largest, most complex brain structure in the animal kingdom.

The reason the PFC is the charioteer-in-chief is because it drives things, including most of the experiences and behaviors filed under the general executive function label. Recall from Chapter 1 that this label comprises a trio of behaviors: response inhibition, cognitive flexibility, and working memory. As we discussed, this behavioral triumvirate can be mixed and matched, wardrobe-style, to produce secondary behaviors like planning, attentional control, problem solving, and emotional regulation. Though scientists disagree on exactly what gets mixed and matched to produce what, they all agree control occurs in here. The PFC drives them all.

Neuroanatomically, you can divide the PFC into several provinces, each with its own behavioral boundary. The lateral PFC (roughly the regions behind the sides of your forehead), is involved in memory formation, attention, and timed sequencing of events. The orbitofrontal cortex (the region right behind your eyes) is involved in response inhibition and social/emotional behaviors. The medial PFC (the region roughly at the crown of your forehead) is involved in conflict resolution, social status updates, and attentional states, too, particularly if a task is challenging. Taken as a whole, the PFC consists of distinct regions, modular in design, each section exerting regulatory responsibility over specific behaviors.[14]

Whether these regions mediate the assigned behaviors outright or are the result of consulting connections is under active investigation. We do know that unusual behaviors arise if you damage the PFC. People can become apathetic. Personalities can change. One famous case from neurological textbooks involves

19th-century railroad construction worker Phineas Gage. An explosion on the job drove a tamping iron through his brain, damaging large regions of the frontal lobe and its connections. Miraculously, Gage survived, but with a personality dramatically altered. The well-liked, responsible worker was transformed into a "fitful, irreverent, indulging" man who was "no longer Gage"— and was soon unemployed.[15]

The Horses

If the PFC is the supervising charioteer, what exactly is the organ trying to manage? Just what a normal chariot-driver manages—the horses, the second component of our metaphor. These behavioral wild stallions lie in the middle of our brain, at the very top of where our spinal cords enter our skulls. This summit goes by lots of names, including "lizard brain" or "reptilian brain," because it functions in us as it functions in lizards and other reptiles. It's the source of our most primitive, violent, "animalistic" emotions.

For all their fierceness and lust, these primitive regions look surprisingly tame, even confectionary—like a benign Tootsie Pop, with an inner core and hard outer shell. The inner core is actually just a swollen region of the spinal cord. It's an important protuberance though, controlling things like breathing, swallowing, heart rate, and blood circulation.[16]

Ballooning above this bulge, and partially surrounding it, is a shell-like group of structures collectively termed the *limbic system*. This system includes regions like the hypothalamus, which controls what behaviorists term "the four Fs": feeding, fighting, fleeing and . . . having sex. The system includes the *amygdala,* which generates and remembers most of the emotions we identify as passions.[17]

Without constraint, these furious appetites would rule our lives, mostly to our detriment. The concept of second-degree murder—an unpremeditated crime of passion—occurs in recognition that some people's wild horses break their connections, then run roughshod over our legal system. The PFCs of these so-called affective murderers don't regulate their lizard brains very well. This means they have a hard time controlling aggressive impulses. It doesn't excuse the crime, of course, but it does underscore the power executive function plays in supposedly civilized society. Interestingly, and perhaps most frighteningly, premeditated murderers have PFCs that bring their internal reptiles to heel just fine; they are the scariest people on Earth.[18]

The Power of the Reins

Connecting the dots between passion and reason is the job of the third component of our analogy: the reins drivers use to control their horses. These connections play the ultimate role in relaying what our rational brains want to say to their irrational cousins. This neurological conversation affects many sectors of our society besides criminal justice. One form even shows up in game shows. The venerable and still-popular TV program *Let's Make a Deal* is oddly similar to an experimental system we use in the lab all the time.

Let's Make a Deal is an over-the-top, frothing-at-the-mouth game show that asks selected contestants to make choices about potentially valuable merchandise. Audience members, festooned in wild costumes, are shown something of worth. They can either keep what they have or trade it in for a (usually obscured) mystery object. The item may be of greater value, like a car; or of lesser value, like a toaster; or in some cases, a gag gift called a "zonk." One famous zonk was a 1965 Volkswagen van dressed to look like a monster, complete with a long red tongue that emerged from its grating with the press of a dashboard button. The appeal of the show is to watch the contestants grapple with perilous bird-in-the-hand-type choices.[19]

This might be hard to believe, but behaviorists use something like *Let's Make a Deal* when measuring aspects of executive function: an experimental protocol called *temporal discounting*. Variations exist, but all involve game show–like options: subjects can choose between taking a small reward immediately or waiting varying lengths of time to receive a larger reward. Unlike the game show, subjects usually know the value of the bigger prize. Whether they're willing to wait for it is the question, making the experiment a measure of impulse control. That's squarely in the wheelhouse of people who study communications between PFC and the limbic structures, the reins of our chariot analogy.

It's tough work. Like a successful Hollywood agent, the PFC's power comes from its connections. Progress has been made understanding the region's complex circuitry, thanks especially to noninvasive imaging techniques. Researchers now know the PFC has three overall classes of connections between it and the rest of the brain (relevant to EF). The first deals with attentional states, the second with stress responses, and the third with general emotional reactivity. Each represents reciprocating two-way conduits in the adult brain, whereby information flows from head to heart and back again. Somehow, responsible behaviors emerge.[20]

Of course, this is a substantial oversimplification, as I frequently explain whenever discussing the rickety bridge between brains and behaviors. To illustrate why I so often choose to oversimplify, let's look at what happens when I *un*simplify, just this once. Below, in italics, find a thoroughly detailed (and thoroughly uninterpreted) description of the neurobiology behind an EF-related behavior: age-related changes in brain activity associated with typical temporal discounting.

Ready?

Maturing impulse control is associated with changes in ventromedial prefrontal cortex activation in concert with alterations in the activation of the posterior parietal cortex, anterior cingulate cortex, ventral striatum, insula, and inferior temporal gyrus. Impulsivity decreases are also associated with alterations in limbic frontostriatal activity, involving networks of neurons associated with inferior parietal cortex, dorsolateral prefrontal cortex, and other less-specified subcortical areas.[21]

Got all that? These are the "reins," dressed in their finest—and most obscure—brain science linen, illustrating just how complex these "reins" can be, even for simple behaviors. Very compelling to a neurobiologist, but hardly a simple affair, which is why this work is so hard to do well.

And it's about to get more complicated. You may not know this, but so far we've limited our discussion mostly to normalized healthy adult Western brains, primarily those of college students and primarily male. Most brain scientists do. Before we leave the topic and get into their teenaged siblings, we have a few confounders to address.

Biased Biology

It's weird to settle in to read a research paper and find yourself chuckling while your entire profession is being marched out to the woodshed. In this case, researchers were taking the entire behavioral research universe to task because of statistical bias in their choice of experimental subjects.

For economic reasons, researchers usually use the cheapest source of experimental subjects available to them: college undergraduates. The subjects are often American (the United States spends more research dollars than any other country), male, relatively well-off financially even when shackled with debt (especially compared to age-matched kids in developing nations), and often white. Detecting bias, the article called our experimental backstops the WEIRDs, short for Western, educated, industrialized, rich, and democratic. The woodshed-escorting data were well reasoned; being clever enough to couch its acrostic in pejorative terms produced the chuckle.[22]

The article makes a knife-sharp point. WEIRD kids aren't representative samples of the total hominid experience. Yet we'll often make pronouncements drawn from our research as if they pertain to the entire human condition, even when all we have to go on are narrow slices of North America.

This is especially hazardous if you consider that the brain has circuit diagrams wired not by nature but by environment. Remember that experience-dependent category we described previously? Brain circuitry isn't always permanently soldered to our neurological motherboards at birth.

This warning certainly applies to executive function research. We know economic conditions can rewire EF's neural substrates, often creating circuits unfriendly to standardized tests. Ditto with stress. And income. A brain might thrive under middle-class conditions, but take that same brain and push its owner below the poverty line, and thriving may not occur at all. The PFC and its relationship to limbic structures are surprisingly vulnerable to how much money you make. We won't explore such confounders further in these pages, but socioeconomic conditions are a legitimate brain issue. It's important to keep all of this in mind—literally.[23]

Similar thin-ice warnings apply to sex- and gender-related issues. We're only beginning to understand how people's place on the gender continuum affects their brain development, or even adult physiology. Here's one embarrassing, fairly recent example: men's and women's brains don't necessarily react to the same drugs identically. That's crucial when formulating, say, medications that keep you from committing suicide.[24] From a sex-based perspective, psychiatric disorders are unevenly represented, too. Schizophrenia is statistically male-heavy, for example, and so is ADHD. Major depression is female-heavy, as is anorexia.[25] These aren't trivial findings. As we'll discover, the age of onset for most mental health issues is *puberty*—and EF plays a central role in many of them.

So, what are we going to do? Since this is a book about science, we have to go where the research dollars have given us streetlights, even if the only view we have is WEIRD. We need to keep these confounders in mind, however, even when it forces us to view certain findings with a great big boulder of salt.

Where We Go Next

I once had a front-row seat to a German protest. I was in Hamburg to deliver a guest lecture, sitting on a street-side bench, eating a sandwich. Suddenly, I heard boisterous noises. A student protest was assembling, and the street filled with young people carrying their signs, anger, and indignation. The students became loud and raucous and mildly threatening. Police looked on from the sidelines, vigilant and *also* mildly threatening.

Like a comet, the crowd soon whooshed past my bench, a gathering ball of noise with a long tail of stragglers, and disappeared around a corner. They were well behaved, fortunately. Minutes later, I noticed one last student, wandering alone with his sign, disorganized and lost. He was intermittently shouting slogans, trying to find his colleagues. The young man began to bristle when he spied a policeman walking toward him. As a lifelong university denizen who has seen many a student protest, I felt sure I was about to see an arrest. Instead, the cop, who was obviously older, touched the young man's shoulder. Smiling slightly, he pointed out to the student where the comet had gone. The young man still gripped his sign hard, but he stopped shouting. He took off in the indicated direction, turned the corner, and disappeared.

The total elapsed time of the incident was maybe 30 seconds, but it spoke volumes to me. Here were two people, one younger, one older, on opposite sides of just about everything in life, including executive function. The teenager had yet to fully develop what many people call maturity and brain scientists might call impulse control—something the older cop had acquired years ago.

We've spent a long time on the cop's side of the brain, talking about his PFC and its mature connections to his lizard brain. Now we need to spend some time with the protestor, whose brain was still in training. Remember, we are trying to solve a mystery—why do some teens act like *Jackass* extras and some act like saints? As long as we keep in mind the confounders just mentioned, there's lots of interesting ground to cover.

3

BRAIN DEVELOPMENT

It's weird to contemplate putting a superhero's cape around an adolescent's neck and thanking that kid for saving the human race. Yet that's what developmental neuroscience teaches us to do. The classic, over-the-top teen temperament has done a lot to keep our species from genetic self-immolation.

What do I mean by "genetic self-immolation"? Consider the Hapsburgs. This royal family held the throne of the Holy Roman Empire from the mid-15th century through the mid-17th century and produced the emperors, kings, and princes of more than a dozen European nations and principalities. Reading the history of this glorious house is like staring in the historical sun—unless you are a geneticist, in which case it's like peering through the window of locked house full of inbreeding cats.

Let's focus on the Spanish branch of the family, who ruled while Spain was at the apogee of its world-conquering prowess and sputtered to extinction in 1700. King Philip I (1478–1506) kicks off the genetic ickiness by marrying his third cousin. That's not so bad, but they have a child who grows up to marry his first cousin. The fruits of *this* marital congress include a second Philip.

Adding to the deleterious heritable baggage, reproductively competent Philip II (ironically called "Philip the Prudent") really dips his feet—and perhaps other organs—into the wells of genetic stupidity. He sires four children with three different close relatives, one of whom is named Mary of Portugal. The child he and Portuguese Mary produce is the third Philip. When less-than-prudent Philip III grows up, he marries yet *another* first cousin.

Got all that? It gets worse. Phil III's son, Philip IV, is the beginning of the end. This terminal Philip creates, with wife Marina (who also happened to be his niece), the sorry genetic masterpiece of this miserable story, the most hapless of Hapsburgs, Charles II. Poor Charlie. He was mentally and physically deficient. He didn't learn to talk until he was 4 or walk before age 8. His parents gave up on giving him an education.

Charles II's physical appearance was closer to something you'd expect to find on a horror movie set than on a European throne. He sported a tongue that was too large for his mouth and so deformed that he could not readily chew his food. He suffered from something historians call the Habsburg Jaw (mandibular prognathism), an excessively protruding lower jaw. He drooled incessantly. He was epileptic. And he was in a lot of pain. Charles II had a combined pituitary hormone deficiency and distal renal tubular acidosis, resulting in excruciating kidney stones. Most important for history, he was sterile, even after swiving through two marriages. Dead before his 40th birthday, he was the end of the Spanish Hapsburg lineage.[1]

Our takeaway: if the only human beings on the planet had been the Habsburgs, there would soon have been no human beings. Just a few generations of consanguineous sex can kill off an entire family.

Fortunately, our species persists—and we have the obnoxious moody behaviors of our youngest reproductive citizens to thank. Good for them. And for us. We'll detail the reasons why it worked out at the end of this chapter. But to get there, we first have to talk about what we know—and what we *used to think we knew*—about brain development.

Myth Busting

It was once thought that brain construction was pretty much complete at birth. Subsequent growth was simply volume expansion, like a balloon blowing up. Pop goes the first myth. We now know that brain development continues long after birth. Indeed, the brain is the *last* organ to mature, not hammering the final neural shingles in place until around age 25 (some researchers think it's closer to 50). Most of these developmental processes are fairly easy to understand, at least in broad terms.

The brain experiences an abundance of growth. In utero, the developing embryo is manufacturing neurons at the hyperactive rate of 500,000 per minute. That pace continues for weeks. If there weren't restraints on the process, human beings might come out of the womb looking like lollipops.

Fortunately, biological brakes exist on this neural exuberance. One type of brake is the most dramatic—cell death. For reasons we only vaguely understand, the embryo's developmental brain program involves killing off cells even while it is manufacturing them. It's kind of like a sculptor, putting large globs of clay on her masterpiece in one area and shaving off smaller bits in another. In the weird world of brain development, doing and overdoing are the same thing.

Another type of brake exists that is probably better compared to a gardener than to an artist. It involves pruning. As discussed in Chapter 2, neurons are social cells and form branching connections with each other almost as soon as they're made. Some connections won't last, just like some cells won't last. Those that survive almost always have their connections trimmed, reconfigured, or both. This pruning in combination with cell death and cell birth constitute the organ's initial developmental processes. And the programmed pruning and reconfiguring continues long after birth.

Some of this programming involves coordinated bursts of neural activity, gradually accumulating like a flash mob in slow motion. Mainly through the work of the late Peter Huttenlocher, who, appropriately, really loved gardening, we now know one burst occurs early, in the first years of life. Connections are formed, trashed, reconfigured, then trashed again. Much of the change involves something called *synaptic density,* a measure of the concentration of neural connections per unit area.

These changes are as uneven as the Alps. Synaptic density in the auditory cortex (where we process hearing) peaks at 3 months, not assuming its adult configuration until puberty. On the other hand, the visual cortex (where we process seeing) peaks later, around 12 months, reaching adult form by age 12. There's lots to do. A typical infant enters the world sporting 2,500 neural connections, but in the next few months, that figure can increase 50 to 60 percent in some of those brain regions.[2]

We used to think coordinated bursts of activity like these ended after the early years, and it's easy to see why. By age 6, the brain is already 95 percent of its adult size. But remember, this is a journey of myth busting. Another burst was discovered to take place amid the hormonal storm surges of puberty. Scientists could see that certain brain regions were experiencing connective growth, similar to what takes place during the early years of brain development, but during puberty, the growth takes place in different regions and at different rates.

We're going to detail this adolescent activity in a few minutes. But I'd like to start with what gets Hurricane Puberty started. The big culprit is a tiny protein whose kindred gene goes by the impossibly funny name *kisspeptin,* originally christened because it was discovered—and I'm not making this up—in Hershey, Pennsylvania, home of Hershey's Kisses.

What do I mean by big culprit? When children reach a certain age, chemicals called gonadotropins fan out from the hypothalamus and start coaxing genitals, neural tissues, and other body parts to begin puberty. Kisspeptin is the protein that tells gonadotropins to start the process. It guides the adolescent developmental program that, for 99 percent of the population, results in the canonical binary of boy and girl.[3]

Interestingly, the timing of the onset of such development is changing. The words "adolescence," "puberty," and "teenager" used to be synonymous, but it's clear now that humans are starting adolescence at earlier and earlier ages. Girls at the close of the 19th century used to start menstruating around age 16 or 17. That figure plummeted to age 12 by 2015, and it's no longer unusual to begin as early as 8 or 9 years of age. Those aren't teenagers; those are 4th graders. Pop goes another assumption.

Why so early? We don't really know, although abundant speculations exist ranging from changes in nutrition to the global use of pesticides.[4] We know only that as kids enter puberty, their brains are being primed to make them the cleverest creatures on the planet—*if* they survive.

Intelligence Matters

It's an extraordinary fact of evolutionary biology that humans took over the world by being smarter, not bigger. Our intelligence allowed us to hunt animals that, in a fair and solely physical fight, would kill us with a quickness. Having big brains ensured there would be no fair fight, even for big competitors.

A case in point is something called a buffalo jump, a clever technique deployed by indigenous peoples of the Great Plains to efficiently slaughter large numbers of bison. Meriwether Lewis, half of the famed Lewis and Clark duo, wrote about it in one of his journals. The technique required only a herd of bison (popularly known to us, and to the Plains Indians themselves, as buffalo) roaming somewhere near a cliff. Bonus points if that cliff had a small crevice or shelf just below it that was big enough for a crouching human.

Several groups of tribal hunters would hide in the grass, positioned behind and beside a large herd. One lone decoy would don a buffalo-hide costume, find a position between the herd and the cliff, and lie down in the grass. On command, the hunter groups would jump up and run toward the herd, startling the animals and making them scatter. The decoy would then pop up as if part of the herd, running in the direction of the cliff. The panicked buffalo would quickly follow. The decoy would pretend to go over the edge of the cliff, but instead tuck himself onto the convenient shelf below. The animals would run full speed over the cliff to their deaths in the valley below. Buffalo jumping was practiced for thousands of years.

Bison outsize and outweigh human beings many times over, but smarter almost always wins over bigger. This is seen not just in generations of clever hunters but also in developing teen brains.

Gray Matter

The first evidence that teen brains develop to be smarter appears in the gray matter, which increases dramatically in adolescence. Recall that these tissues are made up of neuronal cell bodies plus their sprouting, branchlike dendrites. The overall amount of gray matter, thickening like gravy since childhood—creating more dendrites, increasing synaptic density, and expanding connecting options—reaches its maximum at puberty. The peak is at around 11 years of age for girls, 12 for boys. After cresting, the brain goes on a dendritic diet, and a decline in density occurs, mostly through weeding out unused connections and strengthening active ones. This gray matter decline blows over the brain like a wind, starting in the back of the brain and proceeding through the organ until it reaches the frontal lobes, near the forehead. Things don't finish up until the mid-20s.

White Matter

What happens to the surviving neurons? While the quantity of gray matter is rising and falling like interest rates, white matter is also changing. You recall that white matter, made of myelin, is the insulating substance covering nerves the way a plumber's hand might grip a pipe.

Myelination increases over time in adolescents. Given that teens sometimes have all the charm of a root canal, this is a good thing, for myelin assists their brains in taking on more adult functions. Recall that myelin causes neural transmissions to move faster, making them more efficient.[5] Myelin is also involved in what we call neurological refractory periods. After a neuron fires off an electrical signal, it has to wait before it can crack off another signal. This is its refractory period. Myelin helps to shorten that period (30 times shorter than nonmyelinated cells). This increases the readiness of neurons to receive their next electrical assignments, also boosting brain efficiency and assisting teens in their transit from sinner to saint.[6] This boost is not trivial; according to researcher Jay Giedd, whose work was fundamental to these discoveries, the changes result in a "computational bandwidth" increase from infancy to adulthood of about 3,000 fold.[7]

Although no two kids experience these processes identically, it does happen to adolescents all over the world, and roughly in the same order, which is surprising given the also-observed variability.

Linked In

We used to think brain *growth* was the process fueling adolescent brain development—that brains got larger and, therefore, more developed during adolescence. That old fort of an idea has been cheerfully abandoned—thanks to better imaging equipment. The gray matter story revealed by these machines showed that synaptic overgrowth, followed by years of pruning, was the real developmental engine. Similar technology uncovered the primacy of myelination, in which existing connections are made more efficient, by both speeding up the signaling processes and readying them for their next electrical assignments. Taken together, these improvements allowed different regions of the brain to communicate with each other more effectively. According to Jay Giedd, "the adolescent brain does not mature by getting larger; it matures by having its different components become more interconnected and by becoming more specialized."[8]

In a real sense, the teen brain does all this by getting smarter, not bigger. And smarter doesn't just mean growing and pruning cells. There are changes in the way neurotransmitters become available for work, changes in the way their receptors become accessible to greet them, changes in hormones, and differences in the excitability (and inhibition) of neurons and associated neural networks.

Although these changes happen in all teenage brains, there's no wholesale neurological goose-stepping. Teens go through this at their own individual paces, as diverse as political points of view. To make matters worse, even specific regions inside a *single* brain go through maturation processes on differing schedules.

Let's look at an example of this mismatch in brain growth by once again returning to ancient Greece, source of our chariot analogy. This time, we'll focus on the mythological story of Phaeton and Apollo, which you may have heard as the story of Phaeton and *Helios* (same story, different name for the sun god). Often it's presented as a cautionary tale about teen impulsiveness, but it unexpectedly provides a solid illustration of teen brain development.

Greek Teenagers

You might recall from your school days that teenage half-mortal Phaethon and full-god Apollo were involved in an Olympian-sized paternity dispute. Phaethon's mother claimed that her kid's dad was Apollo, talented musical surf bum of Greek mythology, whose job it was to drive the Sun on its daily path from horizon to horizon in a mythological chariot pulled by four wild horses. Phaethon, disputed bastard son of the god, wanted proof of paternity. Dear old Dad decided to grant the teen any wish he'd like in order to prove the relationship. For reasons many an American family might understand, Phaethon demanded a chance to drive the family car, otherwise known as the Sun Chariot.

It was a fatal error for the teen. The horses were wild, strong, and capable, but Phaethon wasn't. Too inexperienced, too light, and too emotional, he lost control soon after mounting the chariot. It descended rapidly, flaming Sun scorching the combustible Earth. Farm fields were set afire, rivers evaporated, and cities were reduced to ashes. Zeus, king of the gods, heard the ruckus and put an end to it with a well-placed thunderbolt, which struck Phaethon and killed him instantly.[9]

Tucked into this not-so-delightful story is a neurological illustration concerning human brain development. As before, it involves chariots and a not-so-mythological maturity gap. This time, it leads us to something researchers call the *dual systems model.*

Growth Mismatch

The dual systems model seeks to explain in neurological terms why teens can be such idiots. It hypothesizes that executive-impoverished behavior occurs because of a neurologically timed developmental mismatch. The idea is that certain subcortical structures, like those found in the limbic system, mature first, coming online before the prefrontal cortex is old enough to issue restraining orders (see Figure 3.1).[10] It's the Phaethon story come to life: the horses mature before the charioteer is ready to control them.

A Developmental Gap

Figure 3.1

The dual systems model posits a developmental mismatch in maturational rates between limbic and prefrontal structures.

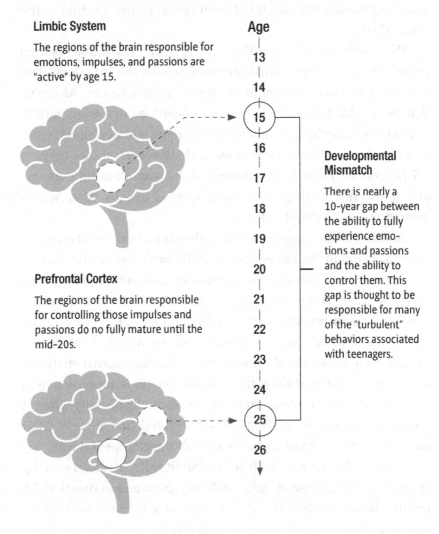

Limbic System

The regions of the brain responsible for emotions, impulses, and passions are "active" by age 15.

Age

13

14

15

16

17

18

19

20

21

22

23

24

25

26

Prefrontal Cortex

The regions of the brain responsible for controlling those impulses and passions do no fully mature until the mid-20s.

Developmental Mismatch

There is nearly a 10-year gap between the ability to fully experience emotions and passions and the ability to control them. This gap is thought to be responsible for many of the "turbulent" behaviors associated with teenagers.

We didn't always think this was the case. For a long time, researchers blamed troubling adolescent behavior mostly on the immaturity of the prefrontal cortex (PFC). As years passed, mounting evidence demonstrated that limbic structures were as involved as the PFC in mediating teen behavior—which meant the original "mono model" needed a fresh coat of paint. The PFC was immature, but in addition, the passion areas were outpacing it in the race to maturity. This juxtaposition created a developmental mismatch between two systems, leading to the term "dual."

We now know that specific regions within the limbic system cross the maturational finish line way before the PFC does. The amygdala is a great example of one of these winners. As we've discussed, this almond-sized organ is involved in a wide variety of affective experiences, including the generation of mood, emotions, and the ability to remember both. Research shows there is a 7 percent increase in the volume of the organ during puberty, and it reaches peak growth rates around age 15, after which growth begins to decelerate.

Another limbic region earning a developmental gold medal is a small region in the lower center of the brain called the *nucleus accumbens* (NA). This knot of neurons helps mediate pleasurable responses and is a primary region involved in addictive behaviors. Its growth trajectory is actually the opposite to that of the amygdala. The NA loses volume—also by about 7 percent—during teen brain development, reaching its growth maturity by shrinking. Interestingly, this smaller region is more active in its reduced state in teens than it is in adults, especially when it comes to risk-taking. It should also be noted that there's a fair amount of controversy about its overall developmental role.

Don't let the words "mature" or "adult form" mislead you. By "mature," I simply mean "fully realizing its intended function." A mature limbic system is still a disorganized, hormone-soaked, maximized mosh pit of passion—something you might well label "immature" observed in its unconstrained form. The 15-year-old "mature" system thus broadcasts "I want to party *now*" signals long before other regions of the brain can muster the desirable response of "Not on a school night, you don't."

So when does the charioteer cross the finish line, mature enough to exert its stern behavioral control over the horses? The answer bids us to leave the hoary world of Greek mythology and turn to the wackier world of Disney cartoons.

Devils and Angels and Kronk

In American cartoons, little shoulder angels and devils are as common as Acme products. My favorite example is from the animated movie *The Emperor's New Groove*, which features a muscle-bound character named Kronk.

Not the sharpest tool in this cartoon shed, Kronk kidnaps the titular emperor, puts him in a sack, and throws him in a river to drown. An off-camera voice says. "You're not just gonna let him die like that, are you?" Then, suddenly, in a poof of animated cliché, a tiny yet beefy Kronk sporting a white robe, halo, and wings appears on Kronk's shoulder. "My shoulder angel!" Kronk declares. Just as suddenly, his shoulder devil, in the form of a tiny red Kronk with horns and a pointy tail, appears in a poof on the other shoulder. "You're not gonna listen to that guy!" the Devil Kronk interjects. "He's trying to lead you down the path of righteousness. I'm going to lead you down the path that *rocks!*" "Oh, come off it," the Angel replies. "*You* come off it," the Devil retorts, and a free-for-all ensues. A conscience-stricken Kronk eventually obeys the shoulder angel, and the emperor survives.[11]

Neural nerd that I am, these good angel/bad angel tropes in cartoons always remind me of my profession, specifically the somewhat anecdotal concept of conscience. Neurologically, "having a conscience" actually involves a maturing, risk-averse prefrontal cortex winning an argument over its more passionate limbic partner.

Considering the previously described mismatch, the mature brain doesn't seem to start out winning. It will *eventually*, when those prefrontals finish changing into their more mature outfits. But the final accessorizing isn't complete until people are in their mid-20s. That's 10 years *after* the limbic structures reach their maturity. Researchers believe this gap between a mature limbic system and still-maturing PFC explains many canonically awkward, even dangerous, teen behaviors. It's the basis for the dual systems model, also sometimes called the developmental mismatch hypothesis.[12]

What exactly does a mature cortical physique look like? And why does the prefrontal cortex take so long to get ripped? It's hard to imagine what good could possibly emerge from a built-in developmental delay that extends bad decision making for another decade. I'll address the second question near the end of this chapter, but I can get to the first one now.

During adolescence, the maturation of the prefrontal cortex's various modules involves putting them on a diet. Measures of gray matter show an impressive 14 percent loss in volume as adolescents transition from high school to the workforce.

Functional connectivity also changes. This occurs in the neural communication lines between the PFC and a self-confident, bossy area of the brain called the *ventral striatum*. The ventral striatum is in a region near the brain's lower center, behind the PFC. It's the part of the system where you feel rewards. It's also involved in telling an overaroused limbic system to shut up. These two functions play critical roles in risk-taking.

By now, you're probably not surprised that neural loss and altered connectivity equate to better function. Recall that maturation involves as much pruning as growing. Recall also that gray matter is composed of cell bodies and connecting branchlike dendrites. It's those dendrites that undergo most of the pruning in a teen's PFC.

Does this maturing have behavioral consequences that can be measured? The answer is a qualified yes, and the clearest example involves revisiting the neuroscience of risk-taking in detail.

A Link Between Brains and Behaviors

One consequence of the gap between cortical brain and limbic brawn is the willingness to take stupid risks. As we've already discussed, teens take risks with such frequency that it's actually a leading cause of death in the age group. This used to puzzle researchers. We know that teenagers are fully capable of making rational, nonrisky decisions, so why do the shoulder devils so often win out over their angelic counterparts?

Added to this mystery is a second finding, which concerns the sometimes lava-hot intensity of teens' feelings. Researchers discovered that teenagers focus more on the potential for *positive* rewards in response to risky decisions than on *negative* consequences. To almost no one's surprise, teens are really into sensation seeking.

Why might that be? One reason is related to something researchers call heightened emotional reactivity. Teen-brain reward centers are more active than children's or adults', making them experience rewards (and other feelings) more intensely than any other time. When they yell out, "I've never been so stoked in my life!" they may be literally telling the truth. And, sadly, perhaps they may never feel that stoked again.

Brain Mapping

You've undoubtedly seen old cartoon posters that map behavioral enthusiasms to regions in the brain. There's the Anatomy of a Man's Brain, Anatomy of a Woman's Brain, Chocolate Lover's Brain, Millennial's Brain, Brains of Boomers, and—relevant to our discussion and my personal favorite—Gary Olsen's "Anatomy of a Teenager's Brain." This one starts off with legitimate names like the prefrontals (correctly identified, even!), but the jokes soon take over. There's the "embarrassed by parents" region, the "ability to remember the lyrics to offensive hip-hop songs" area, the "girls are suddenly fascinating" lobe, and the "have no idea . . ." cortex. Lastly, there's the "school work" area, which the poster describes as being the smallest section of the brain.[13]

Accurate to a funny fault, researchers have tried to do for real what posters like these do for laughs. They've even attempted to map when adult regions like "responsibility for schoolwork" areas start taking over from the "ability to listen to extremely loud bass tracks" regions. Consider an experiment that involved looking at an association between changes in risk-taking and changes in brain development.

The investigators used noninvasive imaging studies in concert with standard assessments of risk-taking behaviors. Their research consisted of "mini-longitudinal" experiments (same subjects followed over time) examining the brain at two age points: (1) before the prefrontals hooked up to limbic structures (average age 15) and (2) after the maturation was in full swing (average age 17). At each point, they examined the tendency to engage in risk-taking behaviors.[14]

What they discovered was an extraordinary snapshot of the brain in the act of being itself, the first of more experiments to come. I should warn you that these are primarily correlational experiments, which don't prove causation. I should also caution that the risk-taking behaviors were not assessed "in the field" but rather in the laboratory, an important variable we'll take up later. To understand these data, we need to briefly review the location of three brain regions, which have more opaque acronyms than a Department of Defense memo.

The first is a module of the PFC called the VLPFC, a region inside the brain midway between the eyes and the ears. The letters VL stand for *ventro-lateral*. The second is also a PFC module, called the MPFC, short for *medial prefrontal cortex*, a region just behind the forehead and above its VL neighbors. The third, which we've already mentioned, is the VS, or ventral striatum, the region known for rewards and stern limbic regulation.

If you look at risk-prone individuals while they're busy deciding whether or not to take a leap off the responsibility cliff (before
age 15), you'll find their VLPFC is lighting up like a Christmas tree
(robust activation). So is their MPFC. In two years, however,
teens begin turning off the holiday lights. Starting at around age
17, a person's VLPFC begins to deactivate itself when there is a
risky choice on the table. The MPFC shows a similar deactiva-
tion, especially in its relationship to the ventral striatum, a correlational decrease also associated with taking less risk.

We think these deactivations constitute the initial construction of a neural pause button. This button will be capable of telling the brain's owner to apply behavioral brakes in the presence
of unwise decisions. It may even be involved in turning down the
volume of "reward sensations," making the stupid less tempting.
Bottom line? Even though such developmental processes aren't
finished until age 20, substantial progress is already developing
in the late teen brain. These remarkable findings are baby steps
in traversing the scientifically rickety bridge between teen brains
and their extraordinary behaviors.

All this is not to say that teens inherit all the wise neurology
they'll ever need to survive by age 17. And not every 17-year-old
shows the maturity revealed in the above experiment, as we've
discussed. Though the general patterns are clear, individual differences remain in both the timing of the neurobiological maturing and its effects on behavior. This lesson was brought home to
me one day while gazing at a yearbook in a rummage sale.

Photographs and X-Ray Eyes

It was an old keepsake from someone's junior high school, and
I had to shake the dust off it before I opened it. The first page I
turned to displayed a photo of the 8th grade class—and some of
the students pictured looked less like 8th graders and more like

5th graders. A scrawny, nerd-in-training boy stood next to a wiry little girl with petri-dish-sized spectacles. Standing beside her was a boy peacocking his obviously well-developed athletic build, ogling the girl in front of him. Or should I say young woman. She appeared more like a soon-to-be senior than a soon-to-be freshman. These kids were all the same chronological age, graduating the same year, but they looked nothing like each other.

There was a simple neurological lesson in that photograph. Though it's convenient to think of adolescent development as everyone experiencing the same events at the same time, that's a fantasy. If we had X-ray eyes and could view every teenager's brain architectures, we'd observe dissimilarities as varied as those in their physical appearance. Researchers find that even in the most robust studies of the dual systems model, only 46 percent of examined teens actually show the developmental mismatch between their prefrontals and their limbic structures. The rest show varying degrees of, well, variation.[15]

This turbulence is made bumpier when researchers address the currently sticky question about whether they are examining boy or girl brains (and exactly what do they mean by "boy" or "girl," anyway?). There are some generalizable observations that withstand the headwinds of individual variation, and, oddly enough, many are gender/sex-related. For example, we know that female brains don't follow the same developmental schedule as male brains.[16] Boys display lower levels of age-matched impulse control than girls and higher levels of sensation-seeking behavior. Females have sensation-seeking behavior, too—in fact, it reaches its peak earlier than in boys—but it also declines more rapidly.[17] For better or worse, both take risks in fairly equal proportions. They just don't get to risk-taking activities by walking down the same developmental trail.[18]

That trail has begun to reveal itself biologically. White matter growth trajectories display sexual dimorphism (sex-based differences), showing structural maturity at earlier ages in females.

Brain regions like the hippocampus and amygdala follow different developmental paths in females. Male brains end up being about 10 percent bigger by volume than females, but growth patterns are wildly uneven. Frontal lobe regions end up larger in females than males, for example. Though no one currently knows whether the behavioral and cellular observations are walking down the same scientific aisle, researchers are looking to see if they're at least dating.

Mental Health

One of the most curious—and serious—aspects of teen brain development concerns mental health, and it's complicated by how we view the sex-based observations just mentioned. Consider a question I often ask my students in lecture: "Do you know the peak onset age for *any* mental health disorder?" And I do mean *any*, either mood disorders (like depression) or thought disorders (like schizophrenia). Nobody ever does.

The peak onset of mental health disorders is 14 years of age. About 50 percent of any mental illness emerges by mid-puberty. By age 24, 75 percent of all mental psychopathologies are in full swing. In my classes, this statement usually engenders a big discussion, because the implications—that most mental health issues may originate in adolescent brain development gone awry—are extraordinary.

Why teens? For the same reasons old 12:00-flashing VCRs used to break down so often: too many moving parts. The wild swings in gray matter and white matter volume, coupled with the unbelievably dynamic brain network changes, are the neurological equivalent of moving parts. Lots can go wrong, and stable mental health may be one of the casualties.[19]

Curiously, psychopathologies afflicting adults look suspiciously like behaviors associated with typical teen *Sturm und Drang*. Wild mood swings, paranoid thoughts, unchecked impulses—all are canonical indicators of adult mood and thought psychopathologies. They are also *de rigueur* for adolescent behavior.

Topping things off, most mental health disorders show explicit sex-based differences. For example, males display antisocial behavior disproportionately to females. Females are more likely to suffer from depression, males from schizophrenia. More females suffer panic disorder. The differences are so robust that noted researcher Thomas Insel declared, "It's pretty difficult to find any single factor that's more predictive for some of these disorders than gender."[20]

When considering these anatomical and behavioral data, the challenges teen brains throw at teen lives become clearer. From individual differences to sex-related behaviors, it's an extraordinarily complex thing to be an adolescent. That's a glib, convenient thing for adults to say, but it underlines a gap in our research. It will be a long time before we'll know how to view the similarities and differences apparent even in musty old yearbooks.

And to add even more complexity, there's a whole other issue. Every kid in any middle or high school class has parents and friends and a social structure probably as bewildering to them as ours is to us. In other words, there is *nurture* to consider, a topic we've so far neglected in this discussion. We'll neglect it no longer.

Lessons from a Frozen Flagpole

A Christmas Story was released in 1983, and over the past few decades, it's ascended to the kind of Holiday Classic status that means it runs on TV in a loop each Yuletide season. In one scene, snarky kid Schwartz, peer group in rapt attendance, double-dog dares gullible kid Flick to touch his tongue to a cold flagpole. Flick doesn't *think* it'll really stick, but he's extremely hesitant to find out. Capitulating to peer pressure when Schwartz *triple*-dog dares him, Flick places his warm tongue on frozen steel and immediately discovers this was a poor choice.

After prying Flick's tongue from the flagpole (with assistance from both fire and police departments), stern teacher Miss Shields tries to get to the bottom of this stupid stunt. Her plan involves strategic peer pressure. "Now I know that some of you put Flick up to this," she accuses, "but he has refused to say who. But those who did it *know* their blame." As she tries to rustle up a confession, tension fills the room. So do smirks. "Don't you feel terrible? Don't you feel remorse?" Miss Shields mourns.

"Adults love to say things like that," the movie's narrator intones, "but kids know better. We knew darn well it was always better not to get caught." They do not rat out Schwartz, and nobody feels terrible about it. The teacher gives up and changes the subject.[21]

That adolescent behavior often differs from the "correct" behaviors adults expect is not surprising. What's surprising is that these behaviors also differ from what adolescents themselves volunteer as being the proper course of action. When decision-making ability is tested in controlled research settings, teenagers go Vulcan—and I don't mean *pon farr* Vulcan. Given hypothetical moral problems to solve, they routinely use—and actually *depend* upon high-level, logical reasoning to guide their choices. They line up the facts that will ultimately guide the decision, and consistently reject subjective, emotional information.[22] Scientists have long known that the ability to reason in a logical fashion matures around mid-adolescence (typically age 15). Rationality is the cognitive showrunner, at least in laboratory situations, making teens every bit the seasoned decision makers that their adult counterparts are.

Not only that, teenagers are fully capable of activating the communication line between their actions and consequences, and you can eavesdrop on this chatter in the laboratory. Observed under specific conditions, adolescents are keenly aware of the cost of their choices. Teens don't *really* think of themselves as "immortal" or immune to serious harm, and they recognize the risk of potentially destructive teen habits, such as cigarette use and unprotected sex. Consider this quote from a research review article, citing the work of Johnson, McCaul, and Klein:[23] "[They] found that adolescents who were daily smokers and those engaged in unprotected sex estimated their risk of getting lung cancer or a sexually transmitted disease, respectively, as significantly higher than others not engaging in those behaviors did."[24]

Why, then, don't teens always choose maturity? This is a central mystery of the dual systems model—a mystery only recently resolved. The answer, interestingly enough, is embedded in the scene from *A Christmas Story*. It turns out that teens' risk-taking is influenced by their psychosocial environment. It is a *nurture* thing, pressurized by the cruel vacuum of peer approval.

Scientists found that they can toggle the quality of teens' responses to choices simply by manipulating the demographics of the immediate social environment. When more adults than peers are in the room, mature decision making wins out, and teens don't yield to triple-dog dares. When more peers than adults are in the room, mature decision making goes out the window, especially regarding risk-taking behavior.[25] That's what I mean by nurture. The neurobiology of a teen's brain may be lab-ready, but whether that teen chooses wise or stupid often depends on how many friends are in sight.

What can we make of this confusing root ball of nature-and-nurture-dependent differences? The current answer, unsatisfyingly, is nothing. They simply demonstrate how many variables we need to understand in persuading teens to keep their tongues off frozen flagpoles.

Darwin and the Aristocracy of Europe

Four months after *A Christmas Story* was released, another cinematic peer-pressure-cooker invaded American movie theaters. *Footloose,* a more grown-up flick, featured a morally conflicted midwestern pastor who condemned dancing because he was convinced the accompanying rock music would lead to adolescent alcohol and drug use and associated debauched dangers. He had a teenaged daughter who wanted to dance anyway. I'm going to use this admittedly dated narrative to illustrate something that isn't dated at all.

Footloose is a cheddar-cheesy movie full of the conflicts typically waged between adults and adolescents. One scene has Pastor Dad explaining to Daughter that her ears just aren't old enough to hear the "adult" things in rock music. Her furious response includes her defiantly screaming that she is no longer a virgin. You can imagine the emotional napalm that follows.[26]

Recall that at the beginning of the chapter I stated that such moody, obnoxious behaviors are responsible for preventing the human race from following a Hapsburgian path to extinction. Let's look more closely at how those two concepts are connected.

As you know, human beings roamed the ancient Serengeti's hazardous obstacle course in small hunter-gatherer groups for millions of years. But imagine what would have happened if the children produced by those small groups interacted solely with each other, the way the European nobility did. You know the answer: they'd end up with a bunch of Charlie IIs. Some would be sterile. Some would become a predator's supper, given their intellectual vulnerability. And humans would hop on the express train to extinction town in a surprisingly few generations.

That didn't happen. And scientists believe the teenage brain was what saved us. Consider: right around the time young humans are becoming reproductively competent, their development makes their familial social interactions increasingly prickly. Nature decided adolescents should turn argumentative, judgmental, and so embarrassed by parental behavior that they wouldn't want any association with them. The result is a firewall of autonomy-seeking behavior so strong that adolescents can't wait to leave the safety of the family group. The familial group, reacting, may be only too happy to see them off. The last thing *either* side wants is to mate with the other.

Bear in mind that "the safety of the family group" is called that for a reason. It's dangerous out there. For our ancestral hunter-gatherers, leaving the social security of the family meant exposure to predation perils, loss of reliable water and food, absence of social assistance—all life-threatening hazards. So nature doubled down and cognitively anesthetized adolescents to the danger. They begin to seek elevated sensations and crave novel stimuli. In other words, they become *teenagers*.

Teens go off to find another hunter-gatherer group and start their mating careers there. This ensures the diversity of the gene pool, saving us from creating Pleistocene Habsburgs. All of a sudden, you have a seriously powerful label for puberty: species savior.[27]

Here's how Jay Giedd couches the evolutionary origins of obnoxious teen behavior:

> [These] behaviors, deeply rooted in biology, and found in all social mammals, encourage tweens and young teens to separate from the comfort and safety of their families to explore new environments and seek outside relationships. These behaviors diminish the likelihood of inbreeding, creating a healthier genetic population.[28]

This is a great business model for species preservation. It solves a problem while simultaneously creating an opportunity. Survival in the hard world of Ngorongoro Crater is the lucrative return on investment.

But the return isn't perfect. While these behaviors are terrifically adapted to life in the ancient Serengeti, what happens when we live elsewhere? Have teen brains adapted to the civilization in which they now reside? The short answer is hardly. There hasn't been enough evolutionary time to convince the teen brain it no longer exists in Pliocene East Africa. This concept has deep implications for the way we teach, parent, and relate to adolescents in the 21st century, and it's to these critical issues that we turn next.

PART III

A BETTER SCHOOL FOR THE TEEN BRAIN:

What Adults Can Do

With executive function's neurobiology addressed, this next pair of chapters circles back to our primary focus: educating teenagers. We'll explore the connective tissue between emotional stability at home and academic performance at school, and we'll review well-regarded, evidence-based parenting practices shown to boost executive function in the adolescents who experience them.

Among the *what-if*'s we'll consider: What if we taught parents about these practices? What if we taught the teachers, too?

4

SAFETY, PARENTING, AND PARENT SUPPORT

Over the decades, futurists have gazed authoritatively into their pedagogical crystal balls and solemnly predicted how students will learn in the future. It's often fun speculation, solemnity notwithstanding. Sadly, very few of their imaginations achieve an escape velocity that can break free of the time in which they live.

One delightfully chilling example is illustrated on a postcard taken from an 1899 collection of futuristic French prognostications. The collection, originally slated to grace the insides of cigar boxes, is titled "En l'a 2000" (a shorthand translation of "In the Year 2000").

The "At School" postcard depicts students seated at tables in a typical late 19th-century classroom. Arcing over the heads of each child are devices looking like a cross between headphones and the leather helmets of the early NFL. On the right stands a wise old professor, busily pouring books into a hopper fixed atop a wire-festooned box the size of a washing machine. The wires connect the box to each child's device. An older student pushes a hand crank on the "washing machine," implying that the book's contents are being electrically force-fed into the pupils' brains. This is no happy Disney version of the world of tomorrow; the students have passive, zombielike looks on their faces.[1]

Although such a rendering evokes steampunk nostalgia, a paean to the 19th century's fascination with all things electrical, predictions from the next century aren't all that much more accurate, even when seriously proposed. In 1958, a Cal Tech researcher envisioned a "push-button" school. Attendance would be taken by students registering their presence by actually pushing buttons. Movies would be the source of direct instruction. "Mechanical tabulating machines" calibrated to each student's individual progress would deliver appropriate content at the push of a button, and students would register their answers by—you guessed it—pushing buttons. Report cards would be generated mechanically and occasionally reviewed by flesh-and-blood teachers.[2]

Even cartoons took a stab at the crystal ball. The very last episode of that animated TV future-fest *The Jetsons* imagined a 2063 version of elementary school. Attended by Jetson's young son Elroy, the school's faculty was populated by robots. Elroy's teacher was a well-intentioned machine named Miss Brainmocker who issued grades on "report tapes." You could hear Elroy say things like, "And eight trillion to the third power times the nuclear hypotenuse equals the total sum of the trigonomic syndrome divided by the supersonic equation," and then hear Miss Brainmocker congratulate little Elroy on his accuracy. Fake facts were allowed to percolate even in this hypothetical neck of the woods.[3]

Humorously imagined or seriously speculated, most of these depictions have one thing in common: a steady dissolution of human-to-human interaction. The 19th century reduced the sage to someone dumping books into a hopper, the mid-20th century to movies and buttons. In contrast, modern cognitive neuroscience reveals that subtracting this critical interpersonal ingredient is done at the students' peril.

From this chapter forward, I am going to take my own shot at describing the ideal school of the future—which I'm designing to be a better school for the teen brain—fortifying my speculations with a large dollop of relational emulsifier. I will do so by asking two focused questions. First, what would a prospective school chock-full of teenagers look like if we seriously addressed issues related to the development of executive function? And second, what would the teacher training look like if it followed the same priority? We are going to connect the neuroscience mentioned in the past few chapters to the American education system, which we've barely mentioned at all. Until now.

Very few educational designs place EF at the center, a neglect that needs to be remedied, given EF's importance to classroom success. Because we don't have a lot of actual data to draw on, our crystal ball is a little cloudy. But that doesn't mean we can't talk about how parts of the school day (and night) might change if brain development related to EF were an essential consideration of educators. From there, we can consider the research necessary to back these efforts and make these changes a reality.

Spoiler alert: there won't be any mention of push buttons in my school of the future. And there darn sure won't be any robots. Sorry, Miss Brainmocker.

Apex Predators

We begin with a blunt-force fact that also sounds like an insult, especially if you're a teacher. Here it is: the brain is not interested in learning. Period. What the brain is interested in is *surviving*. And it is interested in surviving for one powerful evolutionary reason: so that it can advance the genes of its owner into the next generation. Darwinian evolution is the ultimate pre-existing condition for any biological tissue. And, after all, the human brain is biological tissue, following the same evolutionary principles that govern the behavior of sea slugs. It uses learning in the service of survival, not the other way around.

How did our brains acquire this affronting priority? It's here that we run into a contradiction—one that also influences the organization of this chapter.

Humans are the apex predators of Planet Earth, no question. But even a cursory examination of our biological Department of Defense shows we don't deserve the honor. Look at our finger-nails. Not impressive, especially compared to the claws of a lion. Look at our canine teeth. Equally unimpressive, especially con-trasted with those in, say, your standard urban raccoon. Look at our thermal insulation (hair). A gerbil is better adapted to vari-able climate temperatures, clothed as we are in our weak, com-paratively hairless bodies. You'd think we wouldn't be strong enough or big enough to survive the extremely sharp elbows of Pleistocene East Africa.

How, then, did we do it? There are three ways to become king of the hill in the savage world of the *au natural:* you can get bigger, you can get smarter, or you can get smarter in order to *appear* bigger.

The first strategy takes a relatively long time. Turning a mouse-sized elephant into an elephant-sized elephant takes about 24 million generations.[4] The paleontological record sug-gests we didn't wait that long.

There are other ways to double your biomass. Learning to coordinate your behavior with that of another person, say, for the purposes of hunting, effectively doubles your biomass instantly. As long as the two of you remain cooperative, you might very well increase your chances of survival.

Creating positive cooperation also requires creating the concept of "ally." This means you must form a steady relation-ship with another person. If you can survive long enough, it's an efficient strategy. You simply have to change the structure/

function of localized brain cells, rather than change the structure/function of myriads of far-flung tissues throughout the body.

That appears to be the strategy humans used. We learned to cooperate, which means we learned to form relationships. We became relationally smarter, which allowed us to appear bigger, which allowed us to take over the world.[5]

Tucked inside this notion are two behavioral bombshells. First, our survival *depended* upon forming positive relationships within a group setting. Most animals didn't take that route, and for interesting budgetary reasons. It takes a tremendous amount of metabolic horsepower to maintain human relationships (we call it "cognitive load"), much larger than, say, remembering where the watering hole is. Many animals couldn't afford it, diverting their energy resources instead into making amazing claws, powerful canines, and insulating fur. We could, apparently. We put everything into our brains, revving up our cognitive engines so we could have a hunting buddy.

This cognitive acceleration increased our ability to process information in many ways, which leads us to our second bombshell: human learning, cognitive though it seems, has its evolutionary roots in *relationships*. Indeed, human learning is primarily a relational proposition. Our ability to create calculus and discover antibiotics is a wonderful recasting of our cognitive talents, but that's hardly their original use. Our Darwinian brain was ever in the service of establishing and maintaining social interactions for the purposes of survival, and it remains so today.

These facts form the scaffolding of our discussion in this chapter. We will explore the association between human learning and human relationships by starting at its trailhead: parenting. Then we'll discuss the linkages between a child's home life and classroom life, which becomes especially important as kids grow into teens. Finally, we'll consider how teachers can work with parents, and how the school of the future should take this relationship seriously.

After all, taking relationships seriously is what allowed us to conquer the world. Then it flew us to the Moon. Surely it can also help us figure out a more effective way to teach the adolescent versions of these smart, dominating hominids.

Freedom from Fear

There are strong developmental bonds connecting home, school, and relational safety. In fact, there's a 1943 illustration that pretty much summarizes them for us. The artwork isn't found in a biology textbook on human anatomy or on a medical school chart. Instead, it's found on an old cover of *The Saturday Evening Post:* a painting by Norman Rockwell titled "Freedom from Fear."

It's the last entry in the "Four Freedoms" series by Rockwell, and it depicts two elementary-age boys sound asleep in their bed. Mom is hovering over them, adjusting their sheets; Dad is standing upright beside her, head down, face worn with concern. He's holding a folded newspaper with headlines silently shouting out the terrors of war, the words "bombing" and "horror" legible to the observer. The painting ostensibly referenced Britain's bombing in World War II, but it could be any war. Or any family.[6]

Even though the sleeping boys possess brains as preoccupied with survival as a frontline soldier's, in the instant depicted, those gnawing instincts are fully satiated by the stable presence of loving family. Although we may not have fully grasped this idea in 1943, the feeling of safety has surprising educational benefits, especially when it comes to academic performance. The reason? Because the emotional climate of a supportive family environment is one of the greatest predictors of a child's executive function abilities. And since you already know how powerfully executive function affects academic success, you can practically predict GPAs of the boys sleeping in the "Freedom from Fear" illustration. They will likely succeed in school—not necessarily because they're smart, and not necessarily because they *are* safe, but because they *feel* safe.

Safety issues are so important for survival that they bully themselves to the front of the line during the opening minutes of an infant's life, inaugurating a process that researchers call *attachment.* Formally stated, attachment is an emotional bond that forms between caregiver and baby. Whether attachment gains admission into Club Stability depends on how consistently an infant's primary needs are addressed. Why is this so important? Because babies come into this world ridiculously helpless. It's in their best interests to lock on to the nearest source of survival, to *attach,* because they're going to need assistance from caregivers for years. If the association with a caregiver is consistent, the baby will feel safe, and its brain will latch onto the relationship like a nipple.[7]

Four Quotes to Guide Us

What do safety and attachment have to do with education? There are hundreds, perhaps even thousands, of research papers published on the relationships among relational safety, parenting, and report cards.[8] Their conclusions, happily, are simple to understand and can be summarized in four tweet-sized quotes authored by professionals who've studied the phenomena for decades.

Here's the first:

> *Parental scaffolding and negative parent-child interactions influence children's academic ability by shaping children's emerging EF.*[9]

Educators reading know that this kind of scaffolding has nothing to do with construction or house painting. Here, the term describes a social interaction between an expert and a novice—a teacher and a student, or, as in the paper quoted, a caregiver and a child—wherein the novice learns through guided, incremental exposure. The expert begins with the novice's existing fund of knowledge and builds on it by adding something new, usually in bite-sized chunks. This creates a structure—a scaffold—the novice can use to ascend to new conclusions and reach new levels of complex understanding. Parental scaffolding requires a great deal of purposeful interaction between the caregiver and the child.

Three big facts in this tiny quote are worth noting, the first not all that surprising. It states that a child's academic success comes from his or her "emerging" executive function, something I've mentioned before. The second is something we've not yet discussed (though we will later): parental interaction has a profound influence on a child's executive function. The third is that the quality of EF-shaping depends upon the quality of a caregiver's interaction. Negative parental interactions hurt EF development. Scaffolding helps it. This quote summarizes the direct effects of parenting style on academic performance.[10]

Here's our second quote—pulled from the work of Australian researchers. It asserts that there's a molecular explanation for why positive parenting fosters the development of executive function:

> Highly supportive environments apparently result in lower levels of cortisol, which in turn account for increases in children's EF over time.[11]

Stable, positive social environments in the home change how children regulate their stress hormone systems, and stress hormone regulation has a direct effect on executive function development. One of the most studied of these hormones is the glucocorticoid *cortisol,* the famous signal-caller of the HPA (hypothalamic-pituitary-adrenal) stress system. Kids in relationally safe homes have more robust executive function ability because they consistently experience lower stress hormone levels. That's educationally important. In addition to flagrantly fouling EF, excess stress can damage specific regions of the brain that affect learning—such as the hippocampus.

These data should be written in permanent ink, not the least because they directly affect teenager performance.[12] This leads us to our third quote, taken from research originally done with Latino populations:

> *If anything, important aspects of the home environment are better predictors of adolescent's academic achievement than are features of the school environment.*[13]

What's most notable here is the comparison drawn. Of the two most important inputs in a teenager's educational life, home and school, home is *more* consequential for academic performance. This quote is also important because of its age independence: security is critical not just for little kids but for adolescents, too. Sources of threat come from all points of the social compass, from poverty to bigotry, from parents absent from addiction to parents absent from deportation. Schools aren't supposed to be a substitute for the Department of Health and Human Services—their main job is to teach, after all. But they often end up job-sharing simply because safety plays such an influential role in a teen's success.

Of course, we know from personal living-in-the-world research that security remains important to us long past puberty. We never outgrow our need—or desire—to feel safe.

Our fourth quote is a great illustration of this universality. It comes from the now-deceased (but somehow immortal) public television personality, Fred Rogers, host of the long-running *Mister Rogers' Neighborhood.* It's not exactly tweet-sized, but it earns the extra space:

> *When I was a boy and I would see scary things in the news, my mother would say to me, "Look for the helpers. You will always find people who are helping." To this*

*day, especially in times of disaster, I remember my moth-
er's words and I am always comforted by realizing that
there are still so many helpers—so many caring people
in this world.*[14]

Safety, safety, safety. The brain needs a constant supply of safety as surely as it needs oxygen.

Parenting Styles

How, then, given the importance of safety, safety, safety, should parents act to provide the most reassurance for their children? And why is it important for educators to examine such parental behaviors?

We'll address the second question after we've explored a detailed answer to the first. Surprisingly, it's possible to get granular, behaviorally precise answers concerning safety even when studying the sometimes messy world of parenting. We know about the types of caregiving behavior that optimize security mostly because of the great work of psychologist Diana Baumrind. Though she did most of her research in the 1960s, her findings (and the ideas behind them) influence fussy researchers to this day.

Baumrind was among the first to show that parenting behaviors in the United States fell into four behavioral clusters. They're often depicted as a four-square grid, reminiscent of Microsoft's corporate logo (see Figure 4.1). The panes of this grid were based on the observation that most parental behaviors had various degrees of "parental responsiveness" (how well the caregiver positively reacted to their children's many needs) and various degrees of "parental demandingness" (how well caregivers communicated/enforced their behavioral expectations).[15] Baumrind showed that only *one* of the four clusters created the behavioral outcomes capable of turning out the highest-functioning kids.

Four Types of Parenting

Figure 4.1

Diana Baumrind's research into parental behavior identified multiple parenting styles, describable in the two dimensions of demandingness and responsiveness. Below is a representation of the styles and how they fit into these two dimensions.

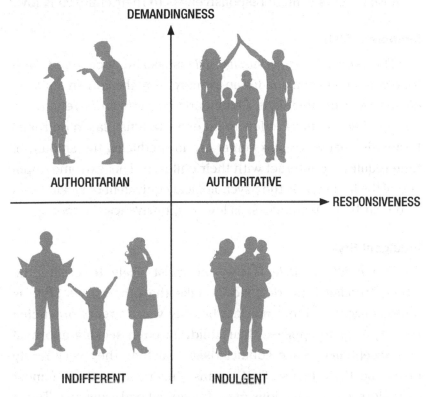

For more information, see Meredith J. Marth, Sonnette M. Bascoe, and Patrick T. Davies, "Family Relationships," in *Encyclopedia of Adolescence*, Vol. 2, ed. B. Bradford Brown and Mitchell J. Prinstein (New York: Academic Press, 2011), 84–94.

While we'll focus mostly on this positive secret sauce, the three suboptimal styles are worth at least a brief mention.

Authoritarian Style

Think of the *authoritarian style* as Mom and Dad meet Marine boot camp. Caregivers following this style display top-down, directive behaviors, with little warmth and lots of punishment. The style is adult-centered and emotionally brittle, with a strong emphasis on rule compliance. Authoritarians possess very little lubricating bilateral communication. Demandingness on the part of these parents is high; responsiveness to their children is low.

Indifferent Style

The *indifferent* or *permissive style* is also adult-centered, with little communication and for an awful reason: the caregivers have disengaged from their kids. Childhood behaviors are barely supervised. Adolescents have few to no expectations placed on them. Permissive parents' goals center around reducing the amount of time required to interact with their children. This extreme opposite of the first style is the psychological equivalent of kicking kids to the curb. Demandingness is low; responsiveness is, too.

Indulgent Style

The *indulgent style* is the one most likely to create the iconic "spoiled little rich kid." Unlike the others, this style is quite kid-centered, but not in a healthy way. Parents practicing this style try to appease their children, often seeking approval and acceptance. Since conflict risks rejection, they very rarely discipline their teens. That means they're accepting of most behaviors, even obnoxious ones. It's not all bad, however. These parents are often quite nurturing and warm. Demandingness is low; responsiveness is high.

There are important caveats to this otherwise fine work. Most of Baumrind's work was done studying heterosexual two-parent households in the United States. With two caregivers, the child receives two parenting inputs, even though the style definitions seem to suggest unitary exposure. As the years have passed, these potential confounders have been addressed (we'll talk about one in a minute), and I'm pleased to say her insights have held up reassuringly well, and in some cases have moved into the rare luxury of settled behavioral law.

Let's move to considering the fourth style: *authoritative parenting*. It produces the type of kid caregivers dream of raising and educators dream of teaching. It gets a deeper dive.

Authoritative Parenting

I remember the moment I realized Diana Baumrind's work had, like a peer-reviewed burglar, crept into my parenting behavior. My sons, 2-year-old Noah and 4-year-old Josh, were engaged in a pillow fight downstairs with our part-time nanny. Noah was learning the hard way about how to use the word "don't" in a sentence, declaring, "Don't stop that!" after a particularly hard hit from big brother. Josh mischievously obliged, replying, "OK!" and then clobbered him twice as hard. "*Don't* stop that!" Noah yelled, exasperated. "*OK!*" Josh roared back, laughing—and hitting him harder. "*Don't stop that!*" Noah shrieked. Nanny tried to intervene as I bounded downstairs. As I inserted myself between Josh and his little brother, he struggled, attempting to continue hitting Noah, and then deliberately bit my hand. He got a major league, terrible, horrible, no good, very bad time-out. Unasked-for physical assault is a big no-no in our household.

So is hanging on to angry feelings. At bedtime that night, Josh got very tender. "I don't want to make a bad choice, Daddy," he said softly. "I don't want to bite you. I don't want to hit you. I love my nice daddy." Then he started crying, "If I bite you, you will have a hole in your hand; then how can you hold anything?"

I gave him a big bear hug, holding back my own tears. I told him I forgave him, that we love him no matter what, and that we were so lucky he was part of our family. I also told him that was the last time he was to bite anyone. He smiled, then went to sleep.

I realized I was doing reps in Baumrind's authoritative gym, the only parenting exercise capable of simultaneously predicting emotional stability and academic performance. I can testify from personal experience that this balance of conditional standards and unconditional love works. Josh is in college now. To my knowledge, he doesn't bite anybody.

I can also testify that authoritative parenting is not for the faint of heart. It not only requires lots of work but also demands emotional dexterity—a balancing act between competing priorities. The "parental demandingness" component requires that parents establish behavioral rules set in titanium, setting clear boundaries and expectations. It also requires equally clear—and consistently applied—punishments for rule infractions.

At the same time, authoritative parents are warm, comforting, and accepting of their children's feelings, just as they are expectant, firm, and consistent toward their children's actions. This is the "parental responsiveness" component of the style. They realize their behavioral standards need to be reasonable, age-appropriate, and, eventually, flexible. It's acceptable to tell Josh not to bite his little brother. It's unreasonable to think saying so will solve all further sibling rivalry issues. Authoritative parents know reflexively how to navigate their children's emotional landscapes the same way they know reflexively how to drive home from work, and they're nice about it the entire time.

The trickiest part comes when kids start aging out of their elementary behaviors and jump helter-skelter into the pyres of puberty. At this point, authoritative parents actively engage with their adolescents in renegotiating household behavioral rules. Discussions begin to focus on issue-oriented decision making, which communicates that the titanium encasing the behavioral rules is capable of melting. It also results in the shifting of compliance responsibility from parent to child. Such controlled surrender is incremental, steady, and focused like a laser on the idea that internalized values and self-directed behaviors make better citizens. The job of parents, after all, is to create kids capable of outlasting them.

Tough as larch wood, this authoritative parenting. And it is just as sturdy. It can be summarized with three characteristics:[16]

1. *Authoritative parents preserve the best elements of demandingness,* maintaining behavioral rules even at the risk of angering their kids. Yet they're always looking for ways to increase adolescent autonomy and self-direction (see the next characteristic).

2. *Authoritative parents consistently engage their children in verbal consultations,* seldom using the term "because I said so" when renegotiating rules. Instead, they focus on building partnerships. As mentioned, they explain the rationale behind their decisions and show themselves willing to discuss those decisions, regularly asking for teen input.

3. *Authoritative parents preserve the best elements of parental responsiveness,* remaining accessible to their children always and listening with warmth and acceptance (different than approval, by the way). They seem to realize that, regardless of teen reactions, what they do as parents absolutely matters. And what matters most is that the kids know they feel loved—and safe. They are regularly willing to risk their relationship with their teens in the service of a higher behavioral goal. It's the only Darwinian thing to do, after all.

Baumrind Meets Meme

I discovered a terrific illustration of this Darwinian safety dance lurking in an old home-office filing cabinet. The anonymous verbiage might have begun as a newspaper blurb, but it's now found a second life as an internet meme:

> For as long as I live, I will always be your parent first and your friend second. I will stalk you, flip out on you, lecture you, drive you insane, be your worst nightmare, and hunt you down like a bloodhound when I should, because I love you. When you

understand that, I will know you have become a responsible adult. You will never find anyone else in your life who loves, prays, cares, and worries about you more than I do. If you don't mutter under your breath, "I hate you" at least once in your life, I am not doing my job properly.

This Apostles' Creed of parenting has the twin notions of inescapable rules and relentless love. You could easily insert Baumrind's terms "demandingness" and "responsiveness" into its text. And it's backed by years of research, freighted with findings weighty enough to prompt the author of a premier college-level psych textbook to declare, "The evidence favoring authoritative parenting is so strong that some experts have suggested that the question of which type of parenting benefits teenagers the most need not be studied anymore."[17]

That's quite a thing to say, especially given the toughness of the parenting journey. But there are real teeth to this enthusiasm. Authoritative behaviors work so well that teens will experience positive benefits even if only one parent is actively practicing the style.[18]

This good news is about to get even better, especially in relation to classroom behavior. Kids from authoritative households make the best students in almost every way you can measure. Teens raised in these homes are more engaged in classroom discussions than teens who aren't. They have better attendance rates. They have stronger expectations for their overall performance, a behavior critical to success in any student's academic journey. They're the most intellectually adventurous and confident and inquisitive kids in school, too, which also directly affects their grades. Not surprisingly, they're more academically successful than kids raised in any other style.[19]

The good stuff should sound suspiciously familiar to you. These benefits are very much like the academic bling one sees in kids clothed with high executive function scores. This EF apparel can even be observed in the "deficit case" (when authoritative styles are absent). Research demonstrates that the best way to hobble the development of executive function in kids is to *not* parent them in an authoritative fashion. For the worst scores, choose the authoritarian style (Marine boot camp) or permissive style (controlled abdication).[20]

What happens if you teach adults not steeped in the magic of Baumrind's ideas the power of authoritative parenting? These are obviously intervention experiments. Naïve parents of adolescents have indeed been taught how to deploy the demanding/responsiveness elements into their parenting. Sure enough, positive changes in their teens' behaviors are observed, which brings them in line with those who have naturally authoritative parents, especially when compared to untrained controls who aren't at all authoritative naturally.[21]

To put a cognitive cherry on the top of this sweet story, similar positive consequences of authoritative parenting have been observed in other countries—including Iceland, India, China, Israel, Switzerland, and the Czech Republic. The effects on emotional stability and intellectual achievement are incredibly robust. They pop up even when the experiments control for standard socioeconomic status factors.[22]

There is no question that authoritative homes make better students, yet I have a bone to pick with all this good news, especially when it comes to potential genetic confounders. It's a very "nurture" thing to talk about parental interactions, but what about genes? Are there significant inputs from the "nature" side of the field that might help to explain a student's academic successes?

We used to think it trumped all other factors. That now represents an older way of thinking, back when people thought everything was nature versus nurture (as opposed to nature and nurture). Raw ability—inherent intellectual horsepower—is definitely a factor in classroom success.[23] But it's surprising how much the behaviors elicited by authoritative parenting outmuscle sheer intellectual ability in classroom performance. I'm not discounting the effects of nature (I'm a geneticist, after all, and EF, which plays a role here, has a strong genetic pedigree). Nonetheless, the surest way to ensure winning academic gold is to make sure nature and nurture swim in the same positive direction.

Marriage Counseling via Pixar

Let's return to the nurture side of the equation with the description of a developmental/environmental principle found in a Pixar movie: *The Incredibles*. To summarize (for the two of you who haven't yet seen this delightful cinematic confection), Bob and Helen Parr are former superheroes raising three kids. Unbeknownst to his wife, Bob's been sneaking around at night, trying to relive his superhero days. As he tiptoes back home after some clandestine action, he's confronted by Helen.

"I thought you'd be back by 11:00," she says sternly. Bob is deer-in-the-headlights shocked. "I said I'd be back later," he mumbles. She interrupts: "I assumed you'd be back later. If you came back at *all*, you'd be back later!" "Well, I'm *back*," he rejoins, with a flourish of his beefy superhero arms. Helen goes nuclear, and their discussion explodes into a mushroom cloud of shouts. At the argument's peak, they suddenly discover their kids have been listening the whole time. The adults deflate, obviously embarrassed.

"It's OK, kids," Bob says sheepishly. "We're just having a discussion." "Pretty loud discussion," says the daughter. "Yeah, but that's OK," says Bob, with faux fatherly assurance, "because what's important is that Mommy and I are always a team. We're always united against the forces of, uh. . . ." He puts his arm around a reluctant Helen. "Pigheadedness?" she says, giving him an angry look. "I was going to say ego or something like that," he whispers, reconciliation suddenly on his mind. "We're sorry we woke you," Helen says to the kids, "Everything's OK. Go back to bed." They have made it clear to the kids that, though the couple is simmering, their relationship remains intact.

It's a fact as sad as war that sustained marital conflict hurts kids' development. If the nonfictional Bobs and Helens of this world don't resolve their anger, their kids suffer for it at school. We know that when parents are in regular open conflict with one another, behaviors associated with healthy executive function in their kids take a nosedive. So does the kids' ability to get a good night's sleep—and their capacity to fight off infectious disease. The collateral damage hits the classroom. EF, just like sleep and sickness, is tied to academic performance, transforming marital stability into an education issue.[24]

Adult relationships shoulder this weighty learning burden because of those pesky Darwinian safety themes we keep revisiting. Since children's survival is dependent for years on adult caregivers, it's in the child's interest to constantly monitor how the adults are doing. If all's well, pediatric brains develop typically (meaning healthily). If not, pediatric brains develop atypically (meaning unhealthily). Since the majority of couples who have children are also married—though that number is shrinking dramatically—we're talking about the ability of a stable marriage to help create a stable, successful student. Research examining single-parent households, which is woefully underfunded, comparatively, show similar findings. Authoritative parenting, and the safety it brings, exerts comparable behavioral magic in these households, as previously mentioned. A kid's brain is still interested in relational security regardless of the number of adults in the room.

Interestingly, it's not the presence of conflict per se that hurts a child's EF. It's the missed opportunity to also observe conflict-resolving behavior. If children see adults figure out how to stop fighting with the same frequency that they observe adults fight, the kids do just fine.[25] That's why the scene from *The Incredibles* is, well, so incredible. Mom and Dad have a conflict, they resolve that conflict, and the kids witness both. This is the literature's findings illustrated in compact narrative form.

What leads some marriages to win behavioral Academy Awards and others to take home Razzies? We understand in part how long-term relationships work in the United States from the work of famed psychologist John Gottman. An emeritus professor at the University of Washington, John can gaze into his behavioral crystal ball and predict with terrific accuracy which marriages will stay together and which will fall apart. He doesn't really have a crystal ball, of course—just tons of behavioral and physiological data that he's collected over the years. Using tests developed in the so-called love lab, his projections of marital longevity are correct more than 80 percent of the time.[26]

These data reveal that couples descend into the mosh pit of divorce through four predictable steps, observed in the lab through assessments of the couple's conflict-management behaviors. Gottman calls these steps "the four horsemen of the apocalypse":

1. *Conflict turns to criticism.* Couples quit sticking to issues and start attacking each other. Rather than saying, "You didn't put your clothes in the hamper," they say, "You never pick anything up" or "You always expect me to do it."

2. *Criticism turns to contempt.* When such cornering behavior becomes typical, name-calling is not far behind. Regularly calling a partner stupid or lazy, or laughing *at* him or her becomes normal. Consistently communicating derision and disrespect transforms regular criticism into regular contempt. Allies are turning into enemies.

3. *Defensiveness.* Couples locked in these battles raise their emotional shields, of course, and defensiveness becomes reflexive even in emotionally neutral disagreements. They regularly engage in what is termed cross-complaining, with one saying, "You're lazy," and the other responding, "That's not true. *You're* lazy." Or the classic, "Yes, but . . . ."

Healthy adults may cycle through these three behaviors during married life, but in unhealthy relationships, such tactics become their only form of communication. None of these behaviors lead to conflict resolution. All of them lead, silent as death, to the final horseman. When a couple hits this step, you might as well play "Taps":

4. *Stonewalling.* All avenues of connection become exhausted in this sad, terminal stage. Couples quit talking, even leaving the room when the other is present. If communication exists, it takes the form of one-word answers. Marriages at this stage gasp for air, find there is none, then call the lawyers.[27]

Hope amid Despair

Gottman's ability to forecast marital futures had another side to it—one that was much more positive. The collected data not only told him what bad marriages did wrong but also identified what good marriages did right. When examining these Michelin-starred relationships, he found several specific common factors:

1. *Conflict was normal.* Successful marriages often had lots of disagreements.
2. *Positive interactions were also normal, and wildly prevalent.* They outnumbered negative interactions 20 to 1.
3. *While disagreements might be common, attempts to fix relational breaches resulting from conflict were also common.*
4. *The* way *couples resolved conflict was as important as the resolution.* There were optimal styles for conflict in heterosexual couples, with different behavioral tasks for each sex.

The best marriages Gottman studied were populated by women who were willing to openly complain within a particular behavioral envelope. They routinely chose "calm honesty" without criticism or contempt. They registered complaints with an attitude of respect and warmth—not unlike behaviors seen in authoritative parenting.

The best marriages also featured men who willingly received the behavioral opinions of their wives. The husbands made no attempt to devalue their wives' inputs; in fact, they did the opposite, taking their wives seriously, hearing them, and internalizing their remarks.[28] Here's how Gottman described this willingness in a newspaper interview conducted shortly after his findings were published: "We found that only those newlywed men who are accepting of influence from their wives are ending up in happy stable marriages."[29]

Over the years, Gottman and colleagues found these conclusions held steady across a wide range of populations. Successful couples all seemed to follow similar patterns, even in disparate locations, at disparate income levels, or with other sexual orientations. Honest communication, mutual respect, and warmth were capable of forging intimate, interpersonal bonds tough enough to last decades.

So: Is it the case that either a couple has it or they don't? That those who fall short on the communication, respect, and warmth meter are doomed? Happily, no. Gottman's team went on to use their research finding to develop behavioral interventions that would stop couples from summoning the four horsemen. In one powerful study, groups exposed to these interventions dropped their divorce rates by 50 percent![30]

The research world knows how to stabilize marriage, which is an extraordinary thing to say, given the messiness of most human relationships. More people should know the impact of teaching conflict-resolution skills on a developing child's EF. Especially people in the world of education.

Designing a Better School for the Teen Brain

I am now ready to provide my opening proposal for a teen-brain-focused secondary school: a night school annex for parents.

The argument for creating such a program is rooted in a blunt observation: most adults are woefully unprepared to rear children. They have no idea that the marital work of Gottman and the parenting insights of Baumrind are powerful, evidence-based tools that can provide great assistance on the road to creating stable families—and, as a not-so-side effect, to developing well-adjusted, curious, engaged, and academically successful students. To bridge this gap, schools could offer educational courses to every parent who has a child enrolled in the school. These classes would teach a curriculum that's no-nonsense and focused: "How to Improve Your Child's Grades by Creating a Stable Relationship at Home" would teach the Gottman protocols; "How to Become an Authoritative Parent" would teach Baumrind's findings.

These classes wouldn't be parent counseling or marriage therapy; they would be straightforward exercises in information transfer. Night school faculty would be composed of teachers already employed by a district, and, in the ideal world, working at the same school. These personnel would have received professional training in this research and would be well qualified to deliver the information.

How would they obtain this preparation? The Gottman Institute already offers professional training/certification programs that could serve as a model for such courses. There are three levels of practicum training and even a certification track. There are also educational materials that don't lead to certification but certainly describe the work in a detailed fashion. Their methodologies have been formally evaluated and published in peer-reviewed journals, and they come out singing.

Teaching the Baumrind material is not so easily answered, simply because there is no equivalent institute supporting her work. There are websites devoted to fleshing out her findings in detail, but there is no formal certification.

There is a workaround for this problem, however. The solution, which involves a long-term commitment and a fair amount of money, is the subject of our next chapter. Keeping in mind that this is all about the future, we'll address this impracticality—just after I 'fess up to a glaring omission—one that actually affects the practical world.

5

TEACHING WITH EXECUTIVE FUNCTION IN MIND

Stentorian-voiced memoirist and poet Maya Angelou started out in life as Marguerite Johnson. As a young child in segregated St. Louis, she experienced trauma to a degree that is unimaginable for most of us. She found salvation in her relationship with a special teacher named Bertha Flowers. In Mrs. Flowers's eyes, Angelou said, "I was respected not as Mrs. Henderson's grandchild or Bailey's sister but for just being Marguerite Johnson."

Mrs. Flowers was a seasoned educator who believed in young Maya's abilities, challenged her mind, and gave her love and attention that helped her thrive. But Mrs. Flowers's greatest impact was probably on Angelou's most distinctive gift: her voice. Literally.

In her autobiography, Angelou reveals that at age 8, she was raped by her mother's boyfriend. She told. The man, convicted of the crime and given a one-day sentence, was murdered soon after his release. Young Maya concluded that she was to blame. His death was her fault for speaking up. So she stopped speaking, and her silence lasted five years.

Maya was still voluntarily mute when she met Mrs. Flowers, who eventually tired of the little girl's self-imposed vocal embargo. She knew Maya a read a lot and thought a lot—poetry was a big deal—so she started giving her books to read. "You do not love poetry," she said, "not until you speak it." The future Presidential Medal of Freedom honoree responded positively to this attention; sometimes kids need to be reminded their presence is not a problem that needs solving. She heeded Mrs. Flowers's firm exhortations, and by age 13 she was speaking again. The teacher's twin virtues of devotional relationship to Maya's personhood and hard-as-Ozark-granite perspective worked wonders.[1]

Mrs. Flowers had standards, and she was willing to challenge behaviors she considered self-defeating. But she also had warmth—warmth of a power that was capable of nurturing a tremendous talent like Maya's. Perhaps you recognize these factors by their other, more "Baumrindian" names: demandingness and responsiveness. They are the poles holding up the tent of authoritative parenting.

Now, some questions. Does good teaching look like authoritative parenting? If so, should teachers set out to develop these authoritative skills? And specifically: would authoritative teaching improve a teenager's life, perhaps by increasing executive function?

The answers to these questions are the heart of the chapter ahead. Spoiler alert: they are yes, yes, and *yes*.

Of Researchers and Rules

The link between parenting styles and teacher competence has been explored—sometimes unwittingly—by researchers from southeastern Los Angeles to southwestern Rochester. Investigators found the most productive environments, school or home, involved a behavioral choreography of rules and flexibility. Here's a précis of the findings, beginning with the importance of rules.

Researchers found the best teachers consistently gave instructions as clear as acrylic, and just as firm. Teachers began direct instruction activities in a timely manner and ended class on schedule. When students did something right, they got high praise. When they did something wrong, they got firm direction. Either way, feedback was defined, consistent, and usually targeted to the instructor's expectations. Perhaps because of these characteristics, successful teachers spent more of their classroom time on learning activities, rather than on behavior-modification activities. Rules, rules, *rules*.[2]

How does this relate to parenting? One of the hallmarks of authoritative parenting involves establishing consistent behavioral guidelines in the household. Home rules are clearly enunciated and closely monitored. It's a part of the broad spectrum of Baumrind's idea of demandingness, an active ingredient in the magic elixir of high expectations (I'll have more to say about high expectations shortly). Rules are part of good parenting. Rules are part of good teaching, too.

Similarities between competent teaching and parenting are observable by watching the painful negative: what happens when rules are nonexistent or only spottily enforced. Classrooms that are disorganized and have confusing rules, or even nonexistent rules, induce the same behaviors at school that Baumrind's indifferent parenting styles induce at home. When adolescents don't have rules, they're left to the mercies of their still-in-basic-training prefrontals. Relationships suffer at home. Grades suffer at school.

But Not Just Guidelines

It is, of course, possible to go too far with rules.

Consider the totalitarian anecdote from *Battle Hymn of the Tiger Mother,* the book I mentioned in Chapter 1 that recounts parenting behaviors that should sport a warning label. Recall that Amy Chua's daughter was forced to work on her piano piece without food, water, or trips to the bathroom until she perfected it—all under the threat of the dismantling and donation of her cherished dollhouse. As you can imagine, this parenting style received severe criticism from the book's readers.

Like I said, you can go too far with rules. Indeed, research shows teachers who spit out rules with the same frequency at which they breathe aren't the ones who create the more effective learning environments. They reap the unhappy consequences of a dictatorial style of parenting (Baumrind's authoritarian style). This despotic cluster of behaviors is all about control. Obedience is demanded, rules aren't adaptable, and open communication is openly discouraged. This authoritarian style doesn't produce the best-behaved children, and it doesn't produce the best students, either.

Instead of following an authoritarian style, most successful teachers seem to have read the *authoritative* playbook, where every page is inscribed with the word "flexibility." Rules are still acrylic, but there's a tacit recognition that teachers are working with students, not military recruits. Authoritative teachers possess one of the hardest perspectives for adults to achieve with teens: a growing respect for their autonomy.[3]

What does autonomy mean from a research perspective? Scientists define it the way most dictionaries do: "freedom from control or influence; independence." At home, autonomy is the gas tank fueling the uncomfortable switch from unwavering parental loyalty to self-governing adult. In the classroom, it's the switch from unwavering faculty fealty to self-governing independent learner.

Researchers have found that teachers achieving this balance between rules and autonomy oversee the country's most productive classrooms. Students perceive the teacher is increasingly giving them voices—and choices—over certain academic activities. This can include decisions about topics covered and choices about concept discovery. Researchers have draped this feeling in something called self-determination theory. It's a rich tapestry—educational gold, actually—assuming that "inherent in human nature is the propensity to be curious about one's environment and interested in learning and developing one's knowledge."[4]

What we're discussing is an equilibrium between the need for rules and the desire for independence. It's a balance with which authoritative adults—teachers and parents—are very familiar. They work like sweating choreographers to get it right.

Of Diving Boards and Classrooms

There's another component of rule making that is relevant to teaching and practically Dickensian in tone: setting expectations, which the Oxford dictionary defines as "strong belief[s] that something will happen . . . belief[s] that someone will or should achieve something."[5] If we define rules as behaviors for the present, expectations are behaviors for the future.

While surfing the internet once, I came upon an enlightening thank-you card from a student to his teacher. The handwritten text of the card reads, "Dear Mrs. — You are really nice to me and you push me to my goals. Thank you." The words fairly laugh with affection, and the boy who wrote them drew a big heart next to the message.

Below the text are more graphics. He's drawn a diving board. Far below the platform is the word "Goal!!!" The teacher and student are on the board—and she's pushing him over the edge. The panicked student has written "ahh" in the word bubble. The affection is not so obvious here.[6]

Sometimes a picture is worth a thousand peer-reviewed articles, and this drawing is a good example. The student is deeply appreciative, illustrating a warm relationship. But the teacher has clearly enunciated certain expectations and is apparently not shy about communicating them. She is engaging the student, pushing him to make a leap—even though it's scary and despite his reluctance.

For good teachers, expectations are part of demandingness, as integral as fingers are to hands. Clear expectations are part of the authoritative parenting toolkit, too. Is that just a coincidence? Do a teacher's demanding expectations produce academic magic in the classroom like demanding expectations produce behavioral magic at home?

The impact of teacher expectations has been studied in detail, and the answer is a resounding yes. Researchers have known for decades that teachers carrying strong expectations for their students—from rule compliance to academic success—profoundly influence how students perform. Robert Rosenthal's classic 1964 experiment shows this in striking detail.

Typical of so many successful experiments, Rosenthal's work started with a deception. He told some teachers he was giving their students a very special test called the "Harvard Test of Inflected Acquisition." This exam, he said, had a powerful ability to detect which kids were about to experience a dramatic uptick in their intellectual performance. The test did nothing of the kind, of course; it was simply a modified IQ test.

After administering the exam, Rosenthal *randomly* identified certain kids as "the highest scorers," then misleadingly told their teachers that the intellects of this bunch were about to blossom like cherry trees during spring break. Rosenthal then followed the students' progress for two years, and he discovered something amazing. The designation had loaded up the teachers' expectations like sap in a tree. Instructors treated these "special" kids differently, giving them more attention, smiling at them more, and touching them frequently. They provided generous feedback, invariably positive, and allowed them more time than other students to answer questions.[7] The biggest finding was that these expectations affected the students' IQs. As Dr. Rosenthal reported in a NPR interview, "If teachers had been led to expect greater gains in IQ, then increasingly, those kids gained more IQ."[8]

The only variable in the experiment was teacher expectations—but it was enough to change kids' raw intellectual horsepower.

There's a sharp, negative side to these data, unfortunately. Research shows that expectations can hurt teens as well as help them. If a teacher is convinced certain students—for whatever reason—aren't *capable* of doing well, they lower their expectations. The kids feel this and respond by not performing as well. The distressing underbelly of these findings is that socioeconomic factors, from finances to ethnicity, usually play a role in forming a teachers' beliefs. Economically disadvantaged students who fit certain social stereotypes suffer the worst. It's a powerful—and difficult—way of showing the muscularity of demandingness-laden expectations.[9]

It's hard to overestimate the power of these findings. Investigators have been searching for mechanistic explanations. One fruitful area of inquiry posited that expectation formation followed a three-step process, sometimes called DBO (short for *desire, belief, opportunity*). Here's a hypothetical example of how these proposed steps create expectations, beginning with beliefs (in the DBO model, all expectations spring from beliefs).

A teacher wants one of her students to do better in math. After years of working with teens, this teacher is convinced that "students are more capable than they think they are." This belief is a rule, a schema—a way the teacher thinks about her students. From this belief a desire or aspiration is born. Here, it's a wish to improve the progress of a particular student. "I think she can do better in math," the teacher states. The desire creates an opportunity to form an action plan (list of activities) for the student to follow. According to the DBO model, these steps combine to create a motivational force that the student can detect. Improvement follows.[10]

An Active Ingredient

Though now clothed in sophisticated 21st-century statistics, linkages between teacher expectations and student performance have historical roots. The 19th-century poet Johann Wolfgang von Goethe once said, "If I accept you as you are, I will make you worse. However, if I treat you as though you are what you are capable of becoming, I help you become that." Maya Angelou declared something similar almost two centuries later: "Do the best you can until you know better. Then when you know better, do better." Perhaps the best quote is also the most recent, from an anonymous 6-year-old: "My teacher thought I was smarter than I was—so I was."

Achieving this effect requires more than just teachers who act like hybrid uniformed drill sergeants/cheerleaders, however. For expectations to inspire positive change, research shows teachers must first be able to form accurate perceptions of a student's abilities. Behaviorists estimate this accuracy is responsible for about 80 percent of the positive transfer.[11]

Accurate ability assessment obviously requires a teacher to know what makes a student tick. That means possessing a working knowledge of the student's psychological interiors, internal rewards and punishment systems, and intentions and motivations. Mind reading would help. Unfortunately, brains can't do that, except in science fiction movies. Is there a next-best thing?

Happily, there is. There's a psychometric test that researchers can use to measure the ability to evaluate *others'* abilities, and there's a way to improve the skill if the evaluator's aforementioned score turns out to be low.

The cognitive gadget is called Theory of Mind (ToM, also called "mentalizing"). It's the ability to accurately assess and predict the goals, incentives, and belief systems of another person. This awareness includes emotional components, such as understanding things they like, things they hate, and their various personality strengths and weaknesses. It really is all about what makes someone tick.[12] (I'll have much more to say about ToM in Chapter 8.)

The best-characterized psychometric test for mentalizing seems a little creepy. It's the awkwardly named RME test, short for "Reading the Mind in the Eyes." The test was created by Simon Baron-Cohen, a famous cognitive neuroscientist with a surprising family connection: he's the cousin of the comedian and actor Sacha Baron Cohen. To assess mentalizing ability, Dr. Baron-Cohen had subjects look at photographs of the eyes of people experiencing various emotions. The subjects were asked to identify the emotions being experienced. People with strong Theory of Mind can do this easily, scoring high. People who can't identify the emotions score low.[13]

With strong reliability, validity, and reproducibility, the RME test is used in behavioral research laboratories around the world. One consistent finding is that mentalizing is disbursed unevenly across the human family. Some people have a strong ability; some don't. Those with the worst scores are invariably on the autistic spectrum. The question, given this unevenness, is whether it is possible to improve Theory of Mind abilities in typically functioning people.

After much work, the answer turned out to be yes, and the way it's done is surprising—until you think about it, and then it seems like the most natural solution in the world. You do it by having experimental subjects read literary fiction. Five experiments published back-to-back in the prestigious journal *Science* proved this interesting result. Here's what happened:

Subjects were first tested for Theory of Mind ability (using the RME and a few other tests), then asked to read something for a period of time, and then retested for Theory of Mind. Some subjects read high-quality fiction (National Book Award winners), some read nonfiction books, and some read nothing at all. The fiction readers showed terrific improvement in mentalizing scores. Those who read nonfiction (or nothing) showed no improvement at all. (See Figure 5.1 for a graphical summary of the results.) These boosts appeared to be long-lasting. Here's a conservative quote from the paper: "The finding that it is specifically literary fiction that facilitates ToM processes suggests that reading literary fiction may lead to stable improvement in ToM."[14]

These findings generate as many questions as they answer. Even so, they have relevance to our discussion. Part of good authoritative parenting involves clearly delineating expectations. That's also a part of good teaching. Transforming those expectations into academic results depends upon a teacher's ability to

Improving Theory of Mind

Figure 5.1 —

Theory of Mind (ToM) is the ability to accurately assess and predict the goals, incentives, and belief systems of another. ToM can be improved through consistent exposure to high-quality literary fiction.

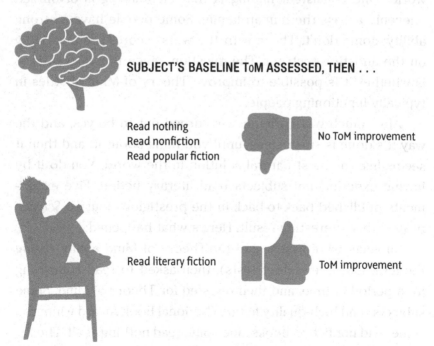

SUBJECT'S BASELINE ToM ASSESSED, THEN . . .

Read nothing
Read nonfiction
Read popular fiction — No ToM improvement

Read literary fiction — ToM improvement

For more information, see David Comer Kidd and Emanuele Castano, "Reading Literary Fiction Improves Theory of Mind," *Science* 342, no. 6156 (2013): 377–80.

accurately perceive student capability. Such accuracy is easily the province of Theory of Mind. Mentalizing is improved by consistent exposure to quality fiction. Does that mean teachers constantly immersed in good literature will improve their accuracy in understanding their student's abilities, and thus their teaching? I have no idea. It is perhaps a research question for another time—although, using my own Theory of Mind, I think I already know the answer.

Not the Only Ingredient

Demandingness is only one of the two dimensions of authoritative skills. The other is responsiveness. Does this dimension play a role in successful teaching the same way it plays a role in successful parenting? The answer to that question is our next subject. And we begin with a sweet example.

Former ice cream company executive and current public schools advocate Jamie Vollmer got more than he bargained for when he compared his world of successful business practice to the practice of education. In a story replete with *mea culpas*, Vollmer recounts a bomb-throwing speech he once gave to teachers about educational reform. This was his opening Molotov: "If I ran my business the way you operate your schools, I wouldn't be in business very long!" He went on to extol the virtue of business, its accountability, and its attention to quality control and wondered aloud why schools couldn't follow his example.

The speech was as popular as an IED. One teacher decided she'd had enough and laid a trap during the Q&A that followed. Starting innocently, she asked about the quality of his company's highly praised blueberry ice cream: "When you are standing on your receiving dock and you see an inferior shipment of blueberries arrive, what do you do?" Vollmer replied, "I send them back."

The teacher pounced: "That's right! And we can never send back our blueberries. We take them big, small, rich, poor, gifted, exceptional, abused, frightened, confident, homeless, rude, and brilliant. We take them with ADHD, junior rheumatoid arthritis, and English as their second language. We take them all! Every one! And that, Mr. Vollmer, is why it's not a business. It's *school!*" Vollmer writes that the teacher had the entire crowd with her, chanting, "Yeah! Blueberries! Blueberries!"[15]

This idea that school is so much more than a business resonates deeply with me, as it apparently also does with researchers investigating the extraordinarily relational components of the job. One topic of interest has been the effects of emotional responsiveness on student outcomes. We're going to discuss the hall-of-fame work of two such researchers, Jacquelynne Eccles and the late Maureen Hallinan.

The Behaviors

The responsiveness side of authoritative parenting declares that feelings don't come with a mute button. It involves two behaviors: the willingness to pay attention to the events in a child's life and the ability to pay that attention with warmth and acceptance. Authoritative parents raise children who become astonishingly loyal to them and to their households. These behaviors also have the benefit of creating internalized compliance to parental admonition. In other words, obedience occurs even when parents aren't around: "I won't make this poor decision because it would really hurt my dad."

Research shows that responsive educators instill something similar in their students, proof that education is not about what kids are taught, but what they learn. Students "attach" to their teachers and, surprisingly, to the whole concept of school, just as they attach to parents and the whole concept of home. One of Notre Dame's franchise educational players, Maureen Hallinan, found three behaviors communicated responsive warmth:

1. *Nonjudgmental interpersonal interactions.* Teachers communicating noncritical, nonjudgmental care got gold stars from Hallinan. Being encouraging, as opposed to being disparaging, without compromising their expectations (talk about a hard balance!) was the ticket. This included respecting a student's family and peer relationships.

2. *Fairness.* Teachers who created consistent rules, doling out rewards and punishments with the fairness of Mother Teresa, also communicated warmth and respect. We previously discussed this behavior in the demandingness section, but it belongs here, too, and for a surprising reason. Such impartiality translates into safety and trust. Teens are as acutely aware of double standards as opposition researchers, after all. Consistency, when present, quickly morphs to warmth.

3. *Praising students for how much effort they put into learning.* Teachers praising a student's intellectual elbow grease, rather than overall performance, also communicated responsiveness.[16]

This last point is reminiscent of Carol Dweck's foundational work, especially her growth mindset "praise ideas," which emphasize cognitive sweat equity over fixed mindset praise. For the few unfamiliar with Dweck's work, here's some advice emblematic of her findings.

If parents want to raise kids who consistently grab academic gold rings, Dweck says to be careful how you praise them. If Cameron gets an *A* on an exam, you're not supposed to say, "Well done, son. You're so *smart.*" The word "smart" appeals to something fixed, immovable. (Dweck actually calls this a *fixed mindset.*) Kids, ever insightful improvisers, then react to getting an *F* by thinking, "I got an *A* because I was so smart. Now I'm failing. It must be because I'm so *dumb.*" They feel as defeated as a pinned insect, and their performance suffers.

Instead, Dweck tells parents to react to Cameron's success this way: "Well done, son. You must have *studied really hard.*" When he fails an exam, he can say, "I got an *A* because I studied hard. Now I'm failing. It must be because I *didn't study hard enough*" and redouble his efforts. Students following this path then feel empowered, and their performance improves. Dweck calls these happy circumstances a *growth mindset.*[17]

The data that students thrive best when their teachers are both demanding and responsive take up the front pews in the First Church of Peer Review.

Of *Playboy* and Parenting

I have had firsthand experience with such authoritative teacher-parenting from my mother, a 4th grade teacher and a wise parent. A case in point was the time I received a 50-megawatt jolt of responsiveness when I was just 13.

I'd found an old *Playboy* magazine in a garbage can and, delighted, stuffed it between the mattresses in my bedroom. Like most teenage boys of the time, I was confident in my bed's ability to cloak my prurient prize. Also like most teenage boys of the time, I had no idea my mother already knew this was an age-worn, teen-worn strategy.

One day after school, with no one home, I went to retrieve my soft-core sin. It was missing! In its place was a little book of sayings, a greeting-card-like tome titled *The Understanding Heart,* inscribed, "Much love, Mom."

I was paralyzed, then horrified. And then I laughed. When Mom came home, I waved her book in the air, trying to appeal to her sense of irony (the book had *really* corny sayings) or redemption—or at least get an explanation. She laughed, too. We had a frank talk about sex, relationships, and the distance between Hefner and Hallmark. My mother's responsiveness bordered on mind reading, which is further evidence of how lucky I was being raised in her household. I still have the book in my office.

The warmth my mother displayed—and the loyalty it strengthened—is typical of parents who practice the responsiveness of authoritative parenting. According to Jacquelynne Eccles, it's typical of teachers who practice it, too.

Dr. Eccles is an iconic psychologist who's done some terrific work navigating the traffic jam between teaching behaviors and student outcomes. Like Hallinan, Eccles observed that responsive teachers inspired student loyalty. Kids were better motivated to learn, leading to more robust classroom engagement, which positively affected attendance. Eccles found that students of authoritative teachers simply liked school more. Students also had better self-esteem when they thought someone was in their lane, cheering them on. They did better in school, unsurprisingly, adding to the deep body of research linking engagement to performance.

Eccles studied how such loyalty programs develop in students' minds. She examined what occurred when students moved from elementary school to junior high—specifically, how student feelings changed about math during the transition. Some had been in elementary classes taught by teachers rated low in responsiveness (not a great start). But if junior high math was taught by highly responsive teachers, these students increasingly attached value to it. Conversely, some students were lucky enough to be taught by elementary teachers rated high in responsiveness. If their junior high math teacher's responsiveness was rated low, unfortunately, the value the students attached to math also suffered. Teachers' authoritative attitudes could turn student attitudes on or off like a switch.[18]

Authoritative parenting and authoritative teaching should take a victory lap together, for they provide astonishingly similar results. In fact, I am going to coin the term "authoritative teaching" as an honorific of the similarities, to describe the educational variant of Baumrind's findings. It's clear that both dimensions of authoritativeness must be present to bequeath the title authoritative teacher onto a given educator. Demandingness improves student grades. Warmth keeps students coming to class. Diana Baumrind would probably give them all a handshake.

No one has formally taught authoritative parenting skills to teachers and then used that instruction as an independent variable to look for its effects on student outcomes (that's something I will suggest at the end of this chapter). But over the years, programs have been developed aimed at improving student-teacher interactions, some with eerie similarities to Baumrind's work.

One such program made it into the journal *Science* a while back. Developed for secondary teachers, it was called MTP-S (My Teaching Partner—Secondary). Teachers videotaped themselves in front of a classroom and sent the tapes to specially trained consultants. The consultants evaluated the tapes, then suggested ways to improve teachers' interactive positivity with their charges. Along with other aspects of the program, MTP-S was tested in a randomized trial involving 78 teachers spread out over a dozen schools and measured for more than a year. The results were a stunner. Assessed the year after the students left the program, student achievement test scores moved from the 50th to 59th percentile—a victory for authoritative teaching advocates.[19]

Proving the Positive with the Negative

What about the other parenting styles? When teachers display Baumrind's less-than-optimal behaviors, do students achieve less-than-optimal outcomes? The answer turns out to be yes, and

I'd like to use the climactic scene from one of the best movies on the subject—*Dead Poets Society*—to illustrate the findings.

The movie boasts a complex plot, but ultimately, it boils down to a prizefight between two teachers and two teaching styles at a private American high school. In one corner is Mr. Keating, played by Robin Williams, who personifies the best of Baumrind's teaching instincts. In the other corner is Mr. Nolan, played by actor Norman Lloyd, who has the teaching instincts of Joseph Stalin. In the movie's climax, Mr. Keating has been fired and Mr. Nolan has taken his place in the classroom. Nolan compels one of Keating's former students to read out loud to the class a treatise on how to analyze poetry. It's boring, rigid, and lifeless as a corpse—which, of course, is the point. There is no joy in this classroom. There is no learning, either.

Before We Leave

Mr. Nolan exhibits a style of teaching behavior that is authoritarian and controlling, and its effects show in the silence of his high school lambs. Mr. Keating's authoritative style, on the other hand, produces curiosity and knowledge transfer and a relational glue that is truly inspiring to watch.

Although Mr. Nolan is fictional, the effect on his students depicted in the movie proves not to be—and there is evidence that Baumrind's indulgent and indifferent parenting styles likewise transfer negatively to teaching.

Hints to this effect have been sprinkled throughout this chapter that they might be; now it's time to be explicit. Educational psychologist Dan Bernstein provides the details, writing on the very subject in a review article a few years back. The article helps to buttress authoritative claims on educational success (though drenched in a whole lot of skeptic-sauce, as I'll relate momentarily). Here are some highlights.

Indulgent Behaviors

As you recall, parents in this model provide few "hard" guide-lines or expectations. Discipline is rare, as is overt confrontation. There's often a lot of affirmation, happily, but it's at a dizzying height. These parents tend to fly behavioral helicopters over every inch of their children's educational landscape.

Indulgent teachers aren't different, Bernstein writes, except for maybe the helicoptering. They tend to be stress-avoidant, overly fearful of damaging a student's self-image, and afraid of flunking anyone. Too much emphasis is given to the student's desire for autonomy, allowing inappropriate control over the way curricula are presented, the way the day is structured, and the way tests are administered. They're as indulgent as a Dove Bar, rewarding students frequently and disciplining them rarely, if at all.

Indifferent Behaviors

Indifferent parents practice a royal abdication of parental responsibility. They don't issue many behavioral edicts, but this is mostly because they can't be bothered. These parents often vote with their feet (they're more absent from their kids' lives than any other style of parent). They also tend to communicate poorly with their teen—they've no practice, after all—providing the behavioral supervision of a middle school hall monitor.

Bernstein writes that indifferent teachers do something simi-lar. There is often very little effort to exert behavioral control; in fact, there is very little effort to exert anything at all. Standards are rare, as is teachers' willingness to explore learning with their students. These teachers present information the same way year after year, covering the same content year after year, most of it rudimentary. The job may be thought of as just a paycheck, and students are certainly viewed as a necessary evil, perhaps in sup-port of that paycheck. Bernstein doesn't say this, but the words "burned out" might be used to describe teachers with such a behavioral profile.

Authoritarian Behaviors

Authoritarian parents can hardly be called neglectful; instead, they tend to have a rigid, dictatorial style of disciplining. They emphasize rules and punishments. Very little open dialogue is expected—or permitted—in such households, and very little warmth is experienced.

Comparable behaviors are observed in teachers who exhibit the same ice-hard style of teaching, according to Bernstein. Expectations are explicitly stated, as are behavioral rules. Teachers displaying an authoritarian style usually provide very little assistance to struggling students. Very little space is given to dialogue, open conversation, or disagreement.[20]

Baumrindian Style and Executive Function

Parenting and teaching styles affect student *outcomes* like yeast affects bread. But what about the mechanisms that produce those outcomes? Are there any hints about the effects of Baumrind's quartet on students' internal neurological machinery—especially as they might relate, say, to executive function? Though the real answer is "we don't know for certain," there are tantalizing clues that most of the good stuff observable in teens occurs because of improvements in EF, and that there are links between parenting and teaching style and EF.

Children raised in authoritative homes display measurably enhanced executive function over children who aren't, as discussed, and the data have recently become as granular as salt. The enhancement is known to occur in two ways: effects have been measured on impulse control (including delayed gratification) and attentional states (including focusing ability). These imprints have real staying power. Effects are still noticeable by the time the kids become teenagers, and they predict both the students' behavioral and academic success.

The behavioral 16-herbs-and-spices turns out to be the degree of controlled autonomy (sometimes called "autonomy support") authoritative parents gave to their children in the first three years of life. Controlled autonomy here means consistently allowing kids choice over specific decisions and letting them take initiative in certain activities. The effects are so powerful they even dwarf the level of parental education.[21]

This boost in EF experienced by children raised in authoritative households suggests some practical ideas for our Better School for the Teen Brain. In this vein, I will offer a few research suggestions (we're going to add to the night classes)—as soon as I address an important reverse-flow issue and get some important caveats off my chest.

The Question in Reverse

What do I mean by a reverse-flow issue? Simply this: a look at the relational current flowing in the other direction. Will a strong teacher practicing authoritative behaviors produce positive effects on the life of a student, even if the student's home life is less than ideal?

This question is, unfortunately, stronger than its answer. There's a tentative "yes," but the supporting research isn't definitive. In general, students under the guidance of teachers who engage and inspire them are buffered against many of the negative effects of a fractured home life, from mental health issues to the ability to handle stress. As Steinberg says, "Students who are engaged in school profit more than just academically from it: It enhances their mental health and protects them against the harmful effects of family problems, stress, and victimization."[22]

Were research in this area to receive higher funding priority, my guess is we'd uncover all kinds of good things. A letter from a young adolescent named Markus (age 11) to Mr. J, his teacher, provides some pointed anecdotal evidence.[23] (Mr. J was so touched by the letter that he posted it online, and it quickly went viral):

> To Mr. J
>
> Thank you for being a awesome teacher and for being amazing! This school year was so fun and I enjoyed it because of you. I wish more teachers was like you. I will never forget you. I look at you like my Dad. I never met my real Dad but it okay because you treat me like im your son. You make me so happy. Always feeding me when I am hungry and hug me when I am sad. I will never forget you Mr. J. I love you and I will never forget about you!
>
> Love Markus

Now, to the caveats.

The Caveats

I've totally left out of this discussion factors relating to genes and statistics. To make things less complicated, I'd like to illustrate these factors with some lively, perhaps apocryphal text messages between a dad and his son. It starts with Dad receiving an emergency text.

> SON: Dad, I got suspended from school.
>
> DAD: WHAT?! Why?!
>
> SON: The teacher pointed a ruler at me and said there is an idiot at the end of this ruler. So I asked which end :)
>
> DAD: You are totally my son!

Dad's response seemed leavened with mirth, and perhaps also with pride.

In the second text exchange, Junior's out in the working world. This conversation also starts with an emergency text.

SON: Hey, Dad, could you lend me $50 for gas while I look for a job?

DAD: Don't you have a job?

SON: I got fired yesterday. My boss told me I needed to leave my problems at the door when I came to work.

DAD: And . . . ?

SON: I told him to go stand outside.

DAD: HAHAHAHAHA! Your mother is going to die when she hears this!

Once again, Dad's response is both unexpected and surprisingly cheery.

What do these interesting texts have to do with what I've omitted? They outline how a kid's familiar behavioral tendencies induce specific reactions in adults—and it's those tendencies I've neglected. As a geneticist, I am only too aware of what Jerome Kagan calls "the long shadow of temperament." Kids' inborn characteristics can deeply influence how they behave and how they learn regardless of how they're taught, which in turn can influence how adults react to them. It sounds like this family has raised a firecracker.

Kagan's work showed that some of these tendencies are inherent, maybe even genetic, and greatly influence the rest of a child's life, even when he or she is no longer a child.[24] Exactly how temperamental characteristics interact with parenting and teaching behaviors is poorly represented in the research literature, sadly, so I've left it out of this research-based discussion. Nevertheless, it is a factor in the real world. Educators know that student temperament matters.

The second caveat is more statistical than genetic: most of the data mentioned here are correlational in nature, not experimental. There's much to be done, including causal work with pre/post randomized trials at its center. This notion means that the suggestions I offer next are best cast as research projects to be explored, which is why I use the word "suggestion" rather than "prescription." These suggestions are based on solid findings; authoritative behaviors in adults *do* link solidly to academic performance in kids, probably because of their impact on executive function. Yet these linkages could use more solid statistical support.

Designing a Better School for the Teen Brain

In an attempt to fill in a gap I mentioned in Chapter 4, my first proposal related to teaching with executive function in mind is a research project that enlists a college of education. You might recall that I advised creating a Night School for Parents that would teach about both Gottman's marital investigations and Baumrind's research. I mentioned that there's a problem teaching Baumrind's research in that, unlike the Gottman Institute, no formal coursework or certification protocol for Diana Baumrind's ideas exists.

That means one needs to be designed, and that's what I propose: create coursework related to parenting/teaching styles and academic outcomes, and administer it through a college of education. Then see how it goes. The coursework should be part of a regular education degree for budding instructors-in-training. Such a curriculum would be perfect thesis work for graduate students interested in exploring the linkages between parenting and teaching in the classroom.

I realize this would take time and money, but there are several advantages to creating such a curriculum. First, newly minted teachers equipped with this training could immediately be recruited to teach the parenting section in our school of the future, for they would know about Baumrind's work, hook, line, and standard deviation. That solves Chapter 4's problem.

But there are other advantages, including creating both social good and a research instrument. The social good comes from the impact of the knowledge on the instructor's personal life. We know statistically that anybody trained in this stuff will make a better parent. Not only will Baumrind-soaked instructors help parents of students attending the schools at which they teach, but they will also benefit personally if they choose to become parents.

Teachers armed with this knowledge will also make also terrific research partners for education scientists, especially those interested in slipping into something more causal. Teachers steeped in "Baumrind sauce" can assist in experimental design and, because they're certified teachers, can provide their classes as research test beds. The Better School for the Teen Brain would thus be buzzing with interactions between real-life classrooms and a local college of education.

Compelling reasons exist to get this research going. To quote educational psychologist Douglas Bernstein directly: "Parenting research, a small number of empirical studies on teaching styles in higher education, and the wisdom accumulated over the years by experienced teachers suggest that an authoritative style is the one most likely to promote student learning, critical thinking, and personal development and least likely to nurture student misbehavior."[25]

Better learning, critical thinking, *and* less misbehavior? I think this is something all parents and all teachers can get behind.

PART IV

A BETTER SCHOOL FOR THE TEEN BRAIN:

What Teens Can Do (and How Adults Can Help)

This final trio of chapters focuses not on adults interacting with teens but on teens interacting with classrooms. How would schools look if enhancing adolescent executive function were their main design features? We'll answer this question by exploring links between EF and a handful of teachable skills: exercise, empathy training, and mindfulness. The discussion illustrates how education systems might practically exploit executive function's steely girders to bridge the gap between our successful elementary schools and our still-the-envy-of-the-world colleges.

The suggestions are a bit unorthodox, granted, but our secondary schools weren't really designed to defend against an attack of the teenage brain. Happily, executive function training, and the work-arounds they suggest, show there's really no need to fight. Bridges, after all, are not offensive weapons.

6

EXERCISE INTEGRATION

The news was bad—really bad. And the fact that it had happened to someone so active and so young made it even worse.

Jason Garstkiewicz was a natural athlete. At age 13, he sported a size-14 shoe and was already 6 feet tall. And he played tons of sports on multiple school teams: football, lacrosse, golf, and basketball (his favorite). An investigation of an injury Jason incurred playing roundball was what led to the really, really bad news: cancer. In four months, Jason would have his right foot amputated along with most of his right leg below the knee.

Experiences like these flatten most people. So you would totally understand if Jason's world fell apart and stayed apart for long, long time. As we've discussed, 13-year-olds are already extremely emotional, more than they will be at any other time in their lives, and they are often more psychologically fragile.

Remarkably, flattening is exactly the opposite of what happened to Jason. According to his dad, Gary, Jason took the news like a trooper—determined, unyielding, and resolute: "[The doctor] gave him options and he was a little emotional in the room for a while, but by the time we got home that night he was on the internet looking at prosthetics and what people who have them can do. . . . It was remarkable how easy he accepted it."

Naturally, there were a myriad of feelings. But for Jason, positivity triumphed. He lost the leg in March of that year, but he was already scrimmaging on the football field with friends a few months later. In less than a year, he was back to lacrosse, playing for the school team and scoring goals with the help of his newly minted prosthetic right leg.[1]

What do we make of Jason? Resident here in a single teenager, we find physical fitness, unexpected resilience, and an emotional steadfastness that might challenge Teddy Roosevelt's. Coincidence? As we are going to discuss in this chapter, the answer is no.

Exploring the brains of people like Jason is one way for us to figure how we might adjust schooling practices to develop more teenagers with his kind of emotional maturity. It won't be easy—there are many complex concepts to cover—but the story is indisputably compelling. And the topic is remarkably well represented in the molecular, cellular, and behavioral brain literature.

The discussion ahead is an extension of the one we've been having, with a new perspective added. For the past two chapters, we've focused on things adults—parents and teachers—can do to foster teenagers' social and academic advancements. In the next three chapters, we're going to discuss things students can do to accomplish the same things. Of course, the adults would still be involved in the sense that we would be the setters of policy and providers of facilities and classes. But it's teens who will be doing the heavy lifting.

Weighty Statistics

Speaking of heavy lifting, there's no question that today's teenagers could do with more regular trips to the gym—*a lot* more.

The U.S. surgeon general found that half of American teens participated in no rigorous exercise program of any kind. Only about 1 in 5 was physically active for more than 20 minutes a day.[2]

Depressingly, the amount of activity kids experience declines as they age out of middle school. The Centers for Disease Control now report that teenage obesity has more than quadrupled since the 1970s. About a third of teens are either overweight or obese. This fact is a gift that keeps on giving: overweight teens tend to become overweight adults. Currently, adult obesity rates stand at 36.5 percent of the American population.[3]

What's odd about these statistics is that we have so many ways to alter them. The exercise equipment industry has come up with exercise technologies designed for virtually anyone at any age to attend to almost any body part. Some seem to have been dreamed up by professional satirists. There's the Shake Weight, a dumbbell that oscillates in a vibrating up-and-down motion. It's supposed to tone your arms, but, at least according to internet comments, it reminds more people of sex than of fitness. There's the Prancercise exercise routine—essentially dancing around the countryside in ankle weights, imitating horse movements from trot to gallop. Continuing with the animal theme, there's even a workout regimen that is literally titled "Work Out Like a Dog." The program consists of a high-octane, interval aerobic workout with rigorous strength training, incorporating a regimen originally designed for our canine friends.[4]

Most of the ads for these exercise "breakthroughs" extol the benefits of "looking good" for the purpose of appealing to the opposite sex. What's missing in these commercials, however, is the benefit exercise has for the organ inside your skull. It's now clear that physical exercise can boost cognition in virtually every way you can measure it. The most surprising thing about these findings is that we reached them not by looking at the brains of teenagers, but by looking at the brains of their grandparents.

Lessons for Teens from Senior Citizens

Initially, researchers were interested in understanding how people's minds performed during aging; learning about how they performed during exercise was just a bonus. In 2001, it was found that CIND (cognitive impairment, no dementia) afflicted more than 15 percent of sedentary senior citizens, but active age-matched controls cut that number by more than half to 6.4 percent. The rate of Alzheimer's disease in sedentary senior citizens was 7.3 percent, but their active colleagues squished that number to a mint-thin 2.2 percent. Generalized dementia of any type afflicted only 4 percent of active seniors, but about 10 percent of sedentary ones. These data showed up even when researchers controlled for the usual whack-a-mole lifestyle variables, like smoking, education, and alcohol consumption.[5]

What in the world was exercise doing for these grandparents? If the secret sauce could be discovered, would it be relevant to their increasingly obese teenaged grandkids?

Researchers suspected something was occurring in the brain chemistry of active populations that wasn't true of people who sat on their butts all day long. Causal findings emerged as the research matured. When a bunch of sedentary people participated in an exercise program for a defined period of time, for example, specific cognitive changes were observed. These newly fit subjects had better memories, better visuospatial abilities, higher reaction speeds, and, important to our discussion, radically improved executive function scores. The best fitness regime turned out to be aerobic exercise.[6]

Direct examination of participants' brains revealed the wizard behind the curtain. Exercise elevated gray matter volume by a whopping 8 percent.[7] It increased functional connectivity between specific neural circuits, wires known for keeping brains as alert as truant children.[8] *And it profoundly increased activity in brain regions responsible for executive function.* Limbic volume (mostly in the hippocampus) increased by almost 2 percent in the brains of the physically active.[9] Exercise positively altered the volume of the PFC (prefrontal cortex), too.[10]

These findings were eventually also confirmed in younger populations. We know that aerobic exercise changes executive function scores in 40-year-olds,[11] for example, as well as in pre-adolescent children.[12] The link between exercise and EF is now as familiar as bottled water.[13]

What about our favorite target audience, the moody, developing teenaged brain? Exercise *does* produce changes in teen EF scores. Exercise has even been shown to dramatically improve grades. But the story isn't simple, and it doesn't work all the time. There are a number of important variables that must be taken into account, because the teen brain is unlike any other brain in the comparative testing categories.

Well, duh.

Inspirational Babysitting

Let's look at those unaccounted-for variables. We begin by showing that these boosts matter to the classroom, even ones clear across the Atlantic Ocean.

Researchers in the United Kingdom found a powerful association between academic performance and moderate-to-vigorous exercise. They even quantified it. For 15- to 16-year-old males, the academic needle began moving with every 17-minute chunk of exercise they performed. For girls the same age, academic benefits showed up at the 12-minute mark. Students who experienced a daily 60-minute dose of sweat could easily improve their performance by a full letter grade. You did not read that wrong. Every 15 minutes of exercise boosted academic performance by a "quarter of a grade." The difference between a *B* and an *A* depended on little more than teens closing books in a class and opening their lungs in a gym.[14]

Such academic observations were observed not only in the British Mothership but in her rowdy former colonies. The most dramatic evidence comes from the research of Michele Tine at Dartmouth College, who works with teens from low-income environments. She found that as little as 12 minutes of daily aerobic exercise exposure boosted their visual attention, the executive gadget that allows brains to ignore competing input and focus on a single stimulus. This improvement resulted in higher reading comprehension scores.[15] Other scientists found similar results, with boosts in different academic subjects. Exercise altered more than just the cognitive side of EF polity, however. Researchers demonstrated gains in the social-emotional aspects of executive function as well. This supports the odd conclusion that if you want more friends, you should make the treadmill your new BFF. Said one researcher, commenting on a meta-review of randomized controlled studies of aerobics in kids through age 12, "[Aerobic physical activity] is positively associated with cognition, academic achievement, behavior, and psychosocial functioning outcomes."[16]

The data are strong enough that one researcher embedded a policy recommendation directly into her peer-reviewed text, proposing legislative changes that would ensure that physical education always survived budget cuts, especially if policymakers really want to boost test scores.[17] I will add in my legislative two cents, too: advocating axing PE time as a way to improve kids' grades is like saying the best way to get a six-pack is to cut out someone's weightlifting class.

Default Network

Unfortunately, aerobic exercise doesn't boost all aspects of teen executive function, and researchers are endeavoring to discover why. Working memory, for example, doesn't seem to be helped by exercise, at least not initially. Yet there are vast changes in how the brain approaches working memory tasks in physically fit kids, and these changes have long-term implications. To understand further, we need to briefly discuss a roped-together series of neurons called the default network.

The default network is conceptually very easy to understand. It's what your brain looks like when you're daydreaming. The network remains active when you're not doing anything else, hence the term "default state." If you become suddenly engaged, the default network is deactivated so that you can reroute resources to focus on the new stimulus. This happens a lot when you decide to remember something. Short-term memory requires the prefrontal cortex and the hippocampus to work together to create the memory. When that happens, they tell the default network to "shut up" (or more accurately, to deactivate) while they focus.

In fit teens, the system works fine. But not in their unfit friends. The default network just doesn't deactivate in their brains like it's supposed to. This causes their hippocampi to work harder than they should. The surface behavior remains intact, and memory scores are the same, but this consistent overdrive is not ideal. And for reasons too complex to explain here, it's something these teens will pay for when they get older.[18]

I should make something clear. If that's all the data on exercise and brain function that were out there, I'd close this section by simply extolling the news that teens need to get off their butts if they want to improve their grades, then move on to the next subject. Unfortunately, that's not entirely true. We have to stay on this topic and get acquainted with the bad news. Not every researcher got the results that Michele Tine and her colleagues did. In fact, some didn't find that exercise had any brain-boosting performance at all.[19]

To explain the discrepancy—and its eventual resolution—we must spend some quality time with an example not from the world of science, but from the world of jazz. Or should I say the world of the movie La La Land, which contains a perfect illustration of the ingredient necessary for teen brains to respond to exercise.

A Lesson in Jazz

I'm not really into musicals, but *La La Land* spoke to me because it's about fulfilling one's dreams. For the character played by Ryan Gosling, that dream is all about jazz. I am a deep admirer of jazz. I actually think it's a brain vitamin, and one particular scene in *La La Land* articulates why.

The scene opens with an embarrassing confession. The lead character, Mia (played by Emma Stone), admits she doesn't like jazz. Seb—that's Gosling—who is a professional jazz pianist, is both offended and challenged. He takes Mia to an L.A. jazz club and begins jazz-mansplaining, as only a purist can, why this form of music is a cultural summit. Jazz is a conversation, Seb says, a relationship that's filled with conflict and compromise, give and take. And it's new every time. One person improvises something, then yields the musical floor to someone else, who then *also* improvises, who then *also yields to someone else.* . . . Seb's enthusiasm for the art form is so obvious you could probably see it from atop the Hollywood sign.

There's a big difference between performing and watching, however, as this scene also delineates. On stage you must be sharp, flexible—anticipating sudden creative outbursts by colleagues, reacting intelligently to constantly shifting, evolving, musical dialogues. Audiences don't have to work those muscles. They can be attentive or passive, grooving the vibe or being distracted, imbibing a solo or imbibing a drink. The cognitive load, not to mention the emotional load, is wildly uneven. You can be in the same room, yet not in the same world.

The Missing Ingredient

Why bring this up? I want to use this movie scene to illustrate the missing ingredient linking body function to executive function.

We begin with a confounder as frustrating as a botched announcement of the 2017 Oscar for Best Picture. As mentioned, the link between aerobic exercise and EF elevation is painfully uneven. Mixed results from competent labs almost always indicate variables exist that haven't been controlled for. Successful labs may have kept the confounders at bay, but it was accidental rather than deliberate. Those labs not fortunate enough to experience the same accident don't get the same result.

Scientists began investigating the troubled relationship between EF and exercise with the methodical discipline of a professional mediator, and they found some possible explanations. For example, if you just engaged in what researcher Adele Diamond calls "mindless exercise"—with no intellectual involvement, no emotional engagement, nothing that matters to gray matter—you reliably got no changes in EF. It was like being in the audience at a jazz concert.

If you added a cognitive component to the exercise, however, engaging the prefrontals of students while simultaneously engaging their muscles, then you got the EF boost other laboratories reported. Such engagement might be accomplished by doing workouts in the context of an organized sport, like basketball or soccer. In these activities, sustained aerobic activity is complemented with simultaneous minute-by-minute improvisations. It's like giving instruments to passive audience members, guiding them to the stage, and letting them improvise. The missing ingredient was in the brain, not in the brawn.[20] (See Figure 6.1.)

These data have been ratified by some timely confirmatory experiments and, in a more granular form, with early adolescents. Using a pre/post design, one experiment tested two types of exercise. The first was garden-variety circuit training, the second an aerobic group game (this group activity required interactive socialization, competition, and motor-based strategic planning). When tested after the intervention, the group players had improved EF scores (working memory, as assessed by a word recall task immediately after their workout)

Exercise and Teen Behavior

Figure 6.1

The presence of exercise-mediated changes in adolescent behavior depends on the type of exercise the teen experiences.

CHANGES IN EXECUTIVE FUNCTION

... are observed when sustained physical activity is accompanied by a strong cognitive component (such as might be experienced in an organized sport).

CHANGES IN RATES OF ADOLESCENT DEPRESSIVE DISORDERS

... are observed with sustained physical activity, whether or not this activity has a strong cognitive component.

compared to those assessed immediately after the circuit training. Engagement did the trick.[21]

Why does this work? Here's Adele Diamond's explanation:

> It may well be that many of the people who maintain better fitness do so by participating in physical activities that involve cognitive challenges. . . . Contrast the disappointing results for aerobic exercise or resistance training without cognitive components with the generally encouraging results for exercise that requires thought, planning, concentration, problem solving, working memory and/or inhibitory control.[22]

Exercise works because the brain is not sitting idly by, like a sideman on break, while the body self-saturates with oxygen. It works because both brain and body can jump onto the stage, strap on their instruments, and start playing their hearts out together.

It Was First Done in Rats

The story about exercise and brains is fun to tell, mostly because the behavioral, cellular, and molecular data all tell a single compelling story. That's rare in my field.

But there's a disclaimer. We've gotten this far not by studying humans but by studying lab animals—mostly rats. Some of the data I'm about to share were first obtained from rodents, and the story is still strongest with them (as you'll see, it's not ethical to do some of this work with humans). It's not a scientific no-fly zone, however. I'm happy to report much of what was observed in animals is also observed in humans, and in a wide variety of ages, including teenagers. Still, rats aren't people, and so the disclaimer needs to be made.

With that in mind, let's look under the hood of this idea and see what the engine looks like. We'll begin with a quote from a research paper that might not make any sense at first, followed by my interpretation of what it says, which I'm praying will be more helpful:

> Brain-derived neurotrophic factor (BDNF) is well known to play an important role in the adult brain in synaptic plasticity learning and neurogenesis, and is considered to be the most important factor upregulated by physical activity.[23]

Let's start with synaptic plasticity, which involves a physiological process that sounds vaguely like a gas additive: LTP, short for *long-term potentiation*.

Plasticity, as we've briefly mentioned, describes the changes that occur in the physical relationships between neurons (activity-based strengthening or weakening of their chemo-electrical relationships, to be specific). These alterations occur when something is being learned.[24] LTP is a specific type of this plasticity. The more flexible the system, the better the learning. The quote above is saying that exercise boosts BDNF, which in turn boosts plasticity.

The quote also mentions a process that sounds almost biblical—*neurogenesis*. *Genesis* means "to create something," and *neuro* means "nerve." So you are creating nerves, or more specifically, new neurons from progenitor cells. This is good news, too. Increased neurogenesis is involved in the potentiation of certain types of memory skills.

The boost is as selective as an Ivy League admissions committee, however. There are only a few places in the brain where neurogenesis can be stimulated after birth. One region is the hippocampus, which you might recall helps convert short-term memories into long-term ones. There are so-called stem cells in parts of the hippocampus, a neural nursery from which neurons can be made.

When you exercise aerobically, you increase *hippocampal* BDNF levels, something this quote neglects to mention. But that's where—and why—the neurogenesis occurs. This elevation affects hippocampal structure, increasing its volume by as much as 2 percent. Not surprisingly, it also increases the ability to acquire and retain information.[25]

How do we know exercise-elevated BDNF fuels intellectual horsepower? The same exercise/BDNF/cognitive increase seen in humans can be seen in rats, and in a more exacting way. If you add BDNF blockers to a rat that is busy exercising, the rat loses its exercise-mediated intellectual boost. Its previous stellar performance on cognitive tests subsequently plummets. These effects are so powerful you can even see this relationship in brain-injured animals.[26]

Is the BDNF story relevant to adolescents, our favorite age group? The answer is yes, but the data were obtained in a slightly different fashion. In a few paragraphs, we're going to talk about how exercise affects adolescent psychiatric disorders, particularly depression. In the teen brain, BDNF plays a powerful role specific to this psychopathology.

Exercise and Blood Vessels

I remember being gobsmacked by my 9th grade science teacher one morning.

The Bell & Howell projector (something that millennial readers might want to Google) was in the room, which meant it was movie time. The gobsmacking came from a comment my teacher made while introducing the film: "The processes you're going to see in a few minutes are so complicated, somebody once said that it'd be easier for a person to be shot out of a cannon—and carve the Lord's Prayer on the head of a pin as he passes that pin—then it would be for this process to occur. Yet it does occur, 16 times a minute on average, every day of your life." Then, with a flourish, he dimmed the lights, started the projector, and for the next hour, we were in the thrall of a movie called *Hemo the Magnificent.*

One in a series of films financed by the old Bell telephone system, this 60-minute educational confection was about our circulation system, complete with animations, cross-sections of living vasculature—red blood cells visible—and what might these days be called a snarky point of view. I was spellbound by the experience, starting with my teacher's comment. And no wonder. The film was directed and produced by none other than Frank Capra, the same Hollywood director who brought the world *Mr. Smith Goes to Washington* and *It's a Wonderful Life.*

The exercising-induced molecule vascular endothelial growth factor (VEGF) would have felt right at home in this extraordinary movie. It has everything to do with creating the blood vessels *Hemo the Magnificent* described that day. The VEGF protein also plays a vital role in understanding why exercise is so good for the brain.

To understand VEGF's academic star power, we first need to discuss the effects of exercise on the brain's cerebrovascular system, the blood vessels winding their way through our heads, like an interstate highway winding through the countryside. They nourish our nerves when they're intact and give us strokes when they're not.

Here's the headliner: aerobics dramatically increases the cerebrovascular density in brain areas important to classroom performance. The hippocampus is one such region.[27] Increased density indicates the presence of more blood vessels, generated via a process called *angiogenesis*. *Genesis* means "creating something," as previously mentioned; *angio* means "related to blood vessels."

The more blood vessels brain tissues acquire, the better those brain tissues function, at least to a point. Why? As you recall from your own high school biology class, blood vessels have the dual function of ferrying supplies and removing waste products. These functions, more complex than can be imagined, were the source of my teacher's enthusiastic prayer-on-a-pinhead comment.

Blood's dual function is a big deal for any tissue, but it's ridiculously important for brains. The reason is that your big, overweight bundle of nerves is an energy hog. Though it's only 2 to 3 percent of your body weight, the brain metabolizes 20 percent of all the energy you ingest. The cerebrovascular system has to have the supply distribution efficiency of Walmart to keep the system running smoothly.

Being the body's quartermaster is hardly the brain's only function. Toxic waste is generated by all this activity and needs to be removed, and that's also been edited into the cerebrovasculature's job description. In the brain, as in most body parts, this human waste comes in the form of unpaired electrons, torn asunder from constituent atoms during energy generation. They don't sound particularly fearsome, but unpaired electrons are really bad actors if left as bachelors. They slam into other molecules, creating dysfunction, sometimes creating cancers, and if left unmolested for five minutes in your head, they can create irreversible brain damage. They really need to go.

This is where Hemo the Magnificent's second function comes to the fore. These trash collectors take an odd form: dissolved oxygen. The gas acts like an electron sponge, sopping up any unpaired charge it finds, then stuffing it into what will become carbon dioxide that you'll eventually breathe out. Trash removal is the reason we need to breathe oxygen.

The more that blood vessels are allowed to penetrate tissues, the healthier those tissues become. This is because energy supplies reach more cells, and toxic waste is more readily removed. That's why increasing blood supplies to areas vital to memory—like the hippocampus—help it to function better. Since aerobic exercise increases the vascularity in learning-critical areas of the brain, most researchers believe this explains why something like regular soccer practice produces cognitive benefits.

The story has increasingly become so detailed that we now have a good handle on the proteins involved in recruiting more blood vessels into the hippocampus. That's where VEGF comes in. VEGF is activated by exercise. It's a protein, therefore encoded by a gene, and exercise has been found to turn it on. This in turn stimulates angiogenesis in brain tissue, creating new blood vessels and increasing branching activity in existing ones. This improves supply routes and waste removal everywhere it's expressed.[28]

Teenage Depression and Exercise

The details of these data have been used to explain more than just effects on a teenager's grade point average. They've been used in an attempt to understand vexing, tough stories like D's story.

D—that's a shortened version of her name—was a teenager interviewed by PBS for a story on teen suicide. She shared that there was a point when almost every experience in her life felt like it was fissuring—school, relationships, family. She began to lose all hope of handling the tension herself, which is a chief herald of a major depressive episode. Unable to find her own way out, D decided that pills could do it for her. She downed seven Advils, one Prozac, and 22 Extra-Strength Tylenols—and went to bed, hoping never to awaken.

But 90 minutes later, she did awaken, and, thankfully, she got cold feet. D tried throwing up, but only blood came out. She tried to alert her parents—she could barely move at the point—by screaming and turned on all the lights she could reach. Dad rushed her to the good doctors at the ER who, after some intense moments, saved her life.

What D didn't count on was how her behavior would seize up her family's life. A willingness to exert permanent solutions in response to temporary problems meant she couldn't be left alone (Dad hauled her mattress into the parents' bedroom). Her sister wouldn't speak to her. No one trusted her, fearful she'd try suicide again. Plus she was scared out of her mind. D was still suicidal a week later, but she also saw what an emotionally ugly thing suicide was to inflict on people who loved her deeply. She promised in her heart not to do it again, which means this story has something of a happy ending.[29]

Many such stories don't. Suicide is the third leading cause of death among kids 10 to 14 years of age, and the second leading cause in the 15 to 34 demographic. Overall, more than 12 percent of teenagers aged 12 to 17 have had at least one major depressive episode of the type that triggered D's pill binge. Teenage girls attempt suicide more often, but teenage boys succeed more frequently, with a suicide rate nearly four times higher.[30] Those who live through the experience have a tough time, for depression generally follows a scorched-Earth policy. Depression, naturally, contributes to poor health, poor grades, and poor social skills. Left untreated, the consequences may be long-term. Depressed teens are much more likely to stay depressed when the teen years are over.[31] With depression, life is a battle hymn sung in a never-ending minor key.

There is good news, especially for kids like D who want out. Depression is very treatable by a variety of measures, a few surprising. It's now clear that the star subject of this chapter, exercise, can exert powerful antidepressant effects. The influence is so strong that the American Psychological Association (APA) recommends mental health professionals make it a major player in a comprehensive treatment regimen. One landmark study showed that rigorous exercise was as successful for treating major depression as antidepressant medications in adult populations. And a follow-up study 12 months later showed that subjects who continued to exercise had a much lower chance of relapse.[32] Exercise can't replace psychotherapy, and it shouldn't be a substitute for taking meds. But the APA is serious when it says that exercise deserves a guest-of-honor place setting at the therapeutic table.

What about our favorite age group? We've made quite an effort to understand that adolescent brains are unlike any other brain at any other age. For one, mental health issues are a big deal to the teenage brain. You might recall that the average age of onset for any mental health issue—including depression—is about 14. There's no guarantee that what is seen in older populations—or younger ones, for that matter—will also be true for adolescents.

Except that in this case, the research shows that the conclusions aren't different. The effects of exercise on adolescent depression have been studied in detail, and the results are good news. One meta-analysis, a collated synthesis of the findings of 11 papers looking at exercise and adolescent depression, came to a singular conclusion. According to lead author Tim Carter,

"Based on our findings, physical exercise appears to be a promising antidepressant strategy for 13- to 17-year-olds."[33]

There are two important aspects to these findings that deserve our attention. First, it didn't seem to matter whether the exercise involved a mindless, robotic workout or an engaging organized sport. Mood was still positively affected, meaning that unlike EF, depression was a less finicky player when it came to letting exercise do its thing. Second, the most powerful effects of exercise programs were observed for those teens whose depression was already being managed by a qualified therapist.

Reassuringly, we're also beginning to understand the molecular mechanisms undergirding exercise and depression relief. Researchers have once again found BDNF to be the signal caller. Depressed individuals were discovered to have severely lowered levels of BDNF, with deficiencies detected in the usual places: the PFC and the hippocampus.[34] The loss was found to be especially severe in suicidal patients. This association has even received a boost from something rare in this patch of behavioral neuroscience: a relevant, human genetic mutation. The mutation is called Val66Met, and people who have it are at a much greater risk for suicide than the general population. Where does that mutation exist? Smack-dab in the middle of the BDNF gene. In fact, the mutation's full name is BDNF Val66Met.[35]

Taken together, we have a maturing story on the effects of exercise on the teen brain. It's strong enough to be obnoxious, and this insufferability can be deployed to make additional recommendations for the kind of school that will best serve teenage learners. We'll do that right after we consider another movie.

Designing a Better School for the Teen Brain

Quest for Fire is a film with an unflinching depiction of the daily life of our Paleolithic ancestors circa 80,000 BCE. I came away from it with three really strong impressions. The first was of the crudity of day-to-day existence, from eating insects to treating wounds. The second was of the constancy of movement. Hunter-gatherers exercised all the time, looking for food, looking for water, and looking for shelter (some researchers believe they used to walk 20 kilometers a day).[36] The third was of the savagery, which reminded me of Thomas Hobbes, who famously described our natural state as "solitary, poor, brutish, and short." Early humans were in constant motion—not just to find sustenance, but to move away from the things that could kill us. And there were lots of things that tried. The upshot is that our big, fat brains grew up under conditions of near-constant motion, for all the important reasons related to just surviving into the next day.

It is this idea that I want to capture as we revisit the Better School for the Teen Brain. Like good narcissists, we've so far focused on brain-based approaches that our own adult age group—parents and teachers—can use to better support teens' education. Now we're looking at what we can do in terms of altering school policies, programs, and bricks-and-mortar design features in order to help teens help themselves.

The physical design of this school is most notable because of what's at its center: a gym. The facility will be in constant use, the hub of the school, in fact. It will be used for general physical education, of course, but this is PE on steroids, if you'll forgive the metaphor. Students will be there every day, and it will function as a research test bed, so that the effects of physical activity on their individual progress can be constantly assessed.

I propose two types of physical activities to fill these needs. The first is mindless aerobic activity as a daily class, something as mandatory as math. Its purpose will not be to get teens in shape but to aid and abet their mental health. This class would be filled with devices for nondisabled populations (like treadmills and spin bikes) and a variety of other aerobic-competent devices for populations with physical disabilities (like handcycles). The second type of activity is organized, cognitively engaging sports. These sports don't have to be the usual suspects (basketball, soccer, track); they could be anything, ranging from Ultimate Frisbee to creative circuit training, as long as the mind tags along. Whereas straightforward aerobic exercise can address depression, the organized sports can address EF issues.

The exercise footprint of this school becomes Godzilla-size in this model. This allows for controlled translational experiments to be performed in real time, answering practical research questions. For example, what if you replaced the desks in classrooms with treadmills and lectured while the students were walking? Would grades improve? It's quite possible that learning is aided and abetted by not allowing blood to pool in ankles and buttocks, as they do in current passive instruction models.

What about movement throughout the day? Should exercise be as constant a presence in a teen's life as french fries? Right now, the system has islands of PE in a sea of sedentary classroom learning. This is contrary to our hunter-gatherer experience in East Africa, where our big, fat brains developed

These ideas are not as far-fetched as they may sound. Schools around the world have embedded daily physical activity into their schedules. By allowing students a 15-minute go-outside-and-play break after every 45 minutes of instruction, Finland's schools keep students active throughout the day. In China, some schools are devoted to a single goal: churning out Olympic-caliber athletes. A group of researchers across the United States developed design specs for school architects, publishing their ideas under the title "Physical Activity Design Guidelines for School Architecture."[37] The Centers for Disease Control has a Physical Education Analysis Tool on their website to help schools design the proper curriculum for implementation of those designs.[38]

The most pointed quality of our Better School for the Teen Brain isn't the presence of a gym, however, but the presence of philosophical shifts. First, we're centering school design around how students *actually* learn. Second, we're performing translational research in a school that also functions as a living laboratory, which is an idea as old as John Dewey.

I realize that what I propose here may not be "practical." Yet impracticality will not change the fact that exercise exerts extraordinary effects on the teen brain. After all, science doesn't aim to please. Science doesn't aim at all.

7

SOCIAL-EMOTIONAL LEARNING

This chapter's topic is social-emotional learning programs and how they influence our plans for the Better School for the Teen Brain. We're going to illustrate this relationship with a nosy, social-emotional peek into a couple of celebrity marriages. Specifically, we'll look at the families of two Bostonian celebrities, Matt Damon and Ben Affleck, childhood friends who brought their mothers to the Oscars the first time they were nominated.

Matt Damon is a rarity in Hollywood. He's been married to the same woman his entire adult life. From the gossip magazine perspective, the couple's prospects didn't seem auspicious. Luciana Barroso was a divorced bartender and a single mom whom Matt had met at a party in Miami, and his friends thought he was crazy to marry her. But marry they did, way back in 2005. It's been a good match. They made a home for Luciana's daughter, then went on to have three more children together. Matt and Luciana are still married and, if the tabloids are to be believed, still very much in love.[1]

Ben's story hasn't been so tidy, and you don't have to read the tabloids to get the picture—just the court filings. He was also married in 2005, to actress Jennifer Garner. They, too, had three children. Ten years later, they publicly announced they were divorcing, and in 2017, the courts made it official. Ben went into treatment for substance abuse (alcohol), a disease that's plagued him much of his adult life. The split has been an amicable experience, if the tabloids are to be believed, and Affleck and Garner share joint custody of the kids.[2]

What do social-emotional learning (SEL) programs have to do with celebrity marriages and the children they produce? Matt's and Ben's families are representative of two experiential sides of American family life: those families who never navigate the rough rapids of divorce and those who do. Social-emotional learning is a factor, because a home's emotional stability profoundly influences teen behavior—and divorce is usually not a sign of stability.

Does exposure to school-based SEL programs help, regardless of which side of the marital continental divide a teen's homestead exists on? More to the point, do SEL programs boost executive function in adolescents? If so, how should this influence our Better School for the Teen Brain design? In Chapter 4, we briefly mentioned what unstable long-term adult relationships can do to a kid's developing mind, but then we spent the rest of the chapter focusing on what to do to help the parents. This chapter is concerned with what can be done at school to help the kids themselves.

Divorce by the Numbers

Divorce has a place in in this conversation because in America, it's as common as potholes. Depending upon how it's measured, about half of all marriages end up disentangling.

Half? *Really?*

You might be surprised to know that there's contention about this number. Some researchers don't agree with 50 percent, saying it's more like 30 percent. Others who accept the

50 percent figure wonder if it's misleading given modern trends and present data showing a declining divorce rate, especially in educated populations. Others disagree with *that* stance, pointing to just-as-recent data showing divorce rates on the rise.

How do we get to the bottom of this? Paul Amato, a research psychologist at Penn State, has been studying the phenomenon of divorce for years. In a 2017 interview with *Psychology Today*, he stated, "If you throw in permanent separations that don't end in divorce, then the overall likelihood of marital disruption is pushing 50 percent."[3] Absent anything better, I'm going with Amato's insights. There is some confirmation bias, however. As of this writing, I've been married 36 years. My wife and I have watched so many of our friends file for divorce that we sometimes think we're on some relational battlefield, watching marriages take hits, stagger to the ground, and bleed to death. It sure feels like half.

What Does That Do to the Kids?

In this book, we are less concerned about what happens to parents than with what happens to their kids. And here the data shout at a decibel level just below a jackhammer. One paper bellowed out the results of two meta-analyses showing that adolescents from divorced households statistically experience more cognitive deficits, suffer more psychosocial shortfalls, and endure more mental health problems than kids from nondivorced ones.[4]

The data get depressingly specific. These kids have greater hostility toward adults (not surprising), are more anxious, are more likely to be depressed and withdrawn, are more aggressive, and have attentional difficulties. They have more problems relating to peers, which means fewer friends, and as a result, are overly sensitive to peer approval. The difference isn't trivial. Adolescents in divorced households are twice as likely to fear peer rejection as kids from stable ones.[5] If some of these deficits sound like the teens need a major tune-up in their executive function engines, you are right on the money.

These problems also reach right into their report cards. If parental divorce occurs in the elementary years, math performance deteriorates, with consequences percolating up into later grades. Predictably, children of divorce score more poorly on standardized tests (both academic and intelligence varieties) than students from stable households.[6]

Some of this, interestingly enough, is due to changes in the family's income. Most divorced households suffer a drop in their standard of living. Not only is there less money to go around, life gets more expensive—especially when factoring legal costs and potential changes in address. Turbulence worsens if moving also means changing schools, disrupting friendships, and losing the familiar daily rhythms of life. All of this upheaval can exert emotionally disorienting negativity at a time when an adolescent's biology is already contributing to the mess. Some kids vote with their feet: students from divorced households are almost three times more likely to become high school dropouts.

There are some important nuances to these data, of course. One is a student's age at the time of the fracture. More long-term negative effects accrue if the divorce occurs in early childhood. Another is the presence of conflict. It isn't *just* the presence of divorce that hurts adolescent minds and hearts. It's the presence of marital conflict that does most of the dirty work. In some households, kids' social and cognitive skills actually *improve* after the divorce process is finished. Divorce is a marker of instability, no question, and from a research perspective a convenient one. But it's not the whole story.[7]

Before leaving this subject, I'd like to address something that may be as personal as your wedding ring. I realize that with marital problems so common, some of you reading this paragraph have already experienced divorce, or soon may. Maybe children were or are involved. You should know my goal here is not to be insensitive toward your circumstances—every divorce is different—but to actually provide good news and a path forward. The effects of such life experiences point to the extraordinary necessity of having SEL programs become a regular part of every adolescent's curricular diet. As we've discussed, emotional regulation really is key to their ability to thrive, and SEL programs help them get there. Statistically, SEL helps many kids—and that may include yours.

So let's get to that good news, focusing on the thriving for a minute. We're going to talk about a behavior measurable when our gangly teens were just babies.

Of Pediatric Heads and Gazes

The behavior is a cognitive gadget called *joint attention*. It's defined as the ability to shift your current focus to something upon which another person is focusing. First observable in 1-year-olds, the phenomenon is famously—and delightfully—illustrated by a three-panel picture.

In the first panel, a mom is seated at a table, baby on her lap. Across from her is a researcher, looking at mom. On a shelf near the table is a brightly colored toy. In the second panel, the researcher turns her head to look at the toy. What does the baby do? It depends on what the researcher does next, which is the subject of the third panel. If the researcher's eyes are open, the baby turns its head and looks at the toy, too. But if the researcher's eyes are closed, the baby won't turn its head. Instead, the baby continues gazing at the researcher.[8]

This is a key finding, and for a developmental reason. If you do that experiment with 9-month-olds, babies turn to the toy whether or not the researcher's eyes are closed (they're following the researcher's head). In three months' time, all that changes. The three-panel experiment shows that the baby no longer follows the researcher's *head,* but rather the researcher's *gaze.* A behavior has been transferred, and maybe even an interest. Now baby and researcher share something, hence the term *joint* attention. It's a powerful way to show how attuned we are, even at early ages, to external social cueing.

We never outgrow this. I see it in adolescents every time a new fashion fad sweeps over the country, with every teen turning their head to attend to the latest sartorial "toy." I see it every time I read statistics about how deeply kids can be affected by busted families. But I also see it somewhere else—in the rising popularity of social-emotional learning. because people in authority, like district leaders, state superintendents, education reformers, and academic researchers, are gazing at them. SEL programs have become popular, and it's for a single, wonderful reason: the best ones work really well. The benefits range from increased social skills to better grades. One meta-analysis showed SEL programs, on average, generate increases of 11 percentile points in academic performance.[9] The reason stems from a principle we've mentioned many times in this book, encapsulated by this quote from a researcher: "Helping kids regulate their emotions can lead to an improvement in their grades . . . even though the intervention has nothing to do with academic achievement. This happens because the self-regulation skills that help control emotions are also helpful for things like studying and homework."[10]

The Structure of SEL Curricula

Most SEL programs have in common certain core competencies (frequently synonymous with executive function skills). Yet some programs work better than others. How can their success be measured and compared? Researchers in the Chicago area were curious, so they performed a meta-analysis, assessing 213 SEL programs from all over the country targeting about 270,000 students in kindergarten through high school.

The researchers found that successful programs shared a quartet of key components: they were *sequenced, active, focused,* and *explicit* (in acronym form, SAFE). This being research, each of these components was carefully defined (in the research paper) as follows:

1. *Sequenced—Does the program use a connected and coordinated set of activities to achieve their objectives relative to skill development?* Programs whose topics were presented in a cumulative fashion and were sequential in nature (unfolding in a step-by-step, elementary-to-advanced order) were more effective than those that didn't.

2. *Active—Does the program use active forms of learning to help youth learn new skills?* Active is just what it sounds like. Rather than having students listen passively to the "sage on the stage," the best programs created plenty of time for participants to take a more immersive, hands-on approach through activities like role-playing and role reversal.

3. *Focused—Does the program have at least one component devoted to developing personal or social skills?* The best programs' content concentrated on *personal* prosocial interactions, not abstract psychological principles. It was taught with the same regularity and the same priority as standard academic subjects like algebra.

4. *Explicit—Does the program target specific SEL skills rather than targeting skills or positive development in general terms?* The best programs focused on specific behaviors within a prosocial framework. Specific topics might include anger management, bullying and perspective taking, or empathy. Empathy was an especially common subject.[11]

These four characteristics were both necessary and sufficient to get SEL programs to fire on all cylinders and achieve related goals, like grade improvement. It seems weird to think that social and emotional safety is an academic issue, but not when you remember that the human brain is more interested in survival than learning. Only when relational security is consistently protected do teachers have a shot at consistently improving academic scores.

Of Deer and Friends

For most teenagers, empathic capacity is not a pre-existing condition, which perhaps explains why teaching it is a challenge. But it's not unheard-of in the species. As a teen, I had learned about it firsthand from a not-too-close friend named Jeff. It was just a little, gentle gesture that he made, but I've never forgotten it.

I grew up as a dependent son in a military family. We lived on numerous Air Force bases, many near undeveloped natural woods riven with trails. I loved those trails. My love was challenged during one spring hike, however, when I nearly crashed into a fully antlered buck moving past me at full gallop. The frightened animal was running from something serious and obviously didn't see me.

I ran back from the trail shaky as a Jenga tower, and when I breathlessly told a group of friends later that night, they all laughed. All except Jeff. He looked at me, puzzled, then unexpectedly said, "You know, if I'd been on that trail, I'd have been scared, too. Those antlers could have poked you right in the eye." I'm not sure if the laughter actually died down, but it seemed to lose volume quickly. Jeff appeared to be trying on my feelings as if they were clothes. He was *empathizing*. I never forgot how good that felt, such sophistication being a rare trait in my friends (and in me, for that matter). It still warms me to think about it all these years later.

Empathy is powerful stuff. It's no wonder that SEL programs have taken a shot at teaching it to adolescents since at least 1979.[12] Empathy plays an outsized role in developing both teens' social cognition and their moral development.[13] Indeed, empathic students have more friends than less charitable kids, and the quality of those friendships is deeper. Researcher Helen Vossen explains, "Empathy enables us to relate to other people. Especially in adolescence, where forming close and meaningful relations with peers is one of the main developmental goals, empathy is an imperative ability to learn."[14]

There's even an academic component to all this behavioral cheerleading: empathy appears to be one of the main qualities associated with grade point changes. It's a stable association between the amount of empathy kids display and their grade point averages (though most of the data remain frustratingly correlative). Students in schools that teach SEL with an empathy emphasis have better reading comprehension scores than those that don't. Why does this happen? Empathy appears to work part of its magic by forcing students to think critically about "other perspectives." This "otherness" translates not just to friendships outside one's own experience, but to concepts outside one's own experience. It promotes cognitive flexibility, which in turn leads to more elaborately conceived—and often quite unique—problem-solving abilities. Reasoning, it seems, involves taking other perspectives. Researcher Delores Gallo writes, "The empirical evidence establishes that it is not just moral reasoning, but reasoning generally which benefits from empathic understanding."[15]

Definitions of Empathy

To understand how this behavioral elixir works, we need to see how researchers characterize its ingredients. Behaviorists divide the definitional world of empathy into two parts. The first is *cognitive empathy,* the ability to take another person's perspective, similar to Theory of Mind skills or even executive function. It's only the *awareness* of someone else's emotional state, however, not the identification with that state. The emotional component is called *affective empathy.* This is the ability to feel vicariously something another person is experiencing. That's what most people think of when they hear the word "empathy."[16]

The brain regions associated with these experiences are well known, demonstrable in research coming from James Coan's lab at the University of Virginia. One very interesting experimental design involves a young adult I'll call Person A, as well as her best friend and a stranger. The brains of both Person A and the best friend are examined via noninvasive imaging (functional magnetic resonance imaging, or fMRI).

The experiment obnoxiously starts with Person A observing her best friend while the best friend endures an electric shock. The shock is not severe enough to cause damage, but it's strong enough to make her bestie very uncomfortable.

Bestie's brain naturally reacts as she experiences the shock. Three regions that mediate normal threat responses become active, which is natural. (These are the *putamen,* the *supramarginal gyrus,* and the *anterior insula,* for you neuroanatomy geeks.)

What happens to Person A's brain, who's merely an eyewitness to the event? The same trio reacts, even though Person A experiences no physical pain at all. Researchers refer to these regions as regions of empathy. Interestingly, if Person A watches a stranger receive those shocks, that empathetic trio of regions never activates—which means that those regions of empathy are not only available but context-dependent.[17]

This is what happens with adults, anyway. Results of similar experiments in teens are very different, underscoring the importance of SEL programs. It is to that subject we turn next.

The Force Is Not Strong with This One

Not to put too fine a point on it, but teenagers are emotional rookies, especially when it comes to empathy and perspective taking. The reason, of course, is that their brains haven't finished developing—the central thesis of this book. Consider, as an example, a love letter[18] from a teen reacting to being romantically rebuffed:

Dear Scout,

You've asked me to stop writing these letters. You've told me they will never change things between us. But I can't, Scout. I can't just . . . let you go. Even Darth Vader, an evil Sith lord, couldn't leave his son to die at the end of *Return of the Jedi*.

You make me feel so safe, Scout. So warm. I want to crawl up inside you. Like Luke Skywalker crawled up inside his tauntaun to protect himself from the sub-zero temperatures of Hoth, where the Rebel Alliance was hiding from the Galactic Empire.

For you, Scout, I would dive into the Sarlacc Pit of Tatooine (Luke's home planet) and be slowly digested for a thousand years, like the bounty hunter Bobba Fett. (Even though in the Expanded Universe of the *Star Wars* novels, Fett eventually escapes, which creator George Lucas has accepted as official S-Dub cannon. But my simile still stands.)

Please, Scout, give you and me a try—or as wise Jedi once said, "Try not. . . . Do, or do not. There is no try." Come on, Scout. Let's "do" it. Let's French. Meet me at Max Brennar this Friday (1/11/13) at 4pm.

Then again, maybe you're right. Maybe we're from different galaxies, far far away from one another. Maybe you're "not the droid" I'm looking for, and I should give up and "move along" . . . with my heart.

May the Force be with You,

P.

Though the author is unknown, he's clearly smitten with this person called "Scout." He's also clearly smitten with *Star Wars*. Scout has asked him to stop writing affectionate notes, but the author can't refrain. Things go from bad to worse, and yes, I'm talking about the author's avowed desire to crawl up inside Scout—not for sex, apparently, but for security, "like Luke

Skywalker crawled up inside his tauntaun to protect himself from the sub-zero temperatures of Hoth."

Much to learn about love, the author still has, for few emotional Jedis exist in the turbulent world of Planet Teenbrain. Which is the point. Researchers have wondered at what age the Force becomes a little stronger in the emotional understanding of adolescents, specifically relationally positive feelings like empathy and perspective taking. Given their measurable importance to factors other than social success—like academic achievement—these are important questions to address.

It's not been easy work. One solid attempt involved a group of Dutch researchers studying the development of teen empathy and perspective taking over a six-year period. The study started with 13-year-olds, tracking the progress of 283 boys and 214 females. For behavioral measures, they used a well-regarded psychometric instrument called the IRI (Interpersonal Reactivity Index), a complex test with numerous subscales. The researchers used the Empathic Concern (EC) subscale to measure empathy and the Perspective Taking (PT) subscale to measure, well, perspective taking.[19]

The researchers were particularly interested in how these key social cognitions developed over time. What they found was interesting, and a great lesson as to why you really have to do this stuff with both males and females.

Empathic Concern and Perspective Taking

The first efforts measured empathic concern, whose developmental trajectory was found to be a bit boring. EC scores didn't change much, with tallies at age 18 roughly at parity with the subjects' younger 13-year-old selves. There were clear differences between the sexes, however. Females consistently scored higher than boys at the beginning of the study, and they maintained those higher levels throughout. In addition, males actually showed a temporary decline in their already-lower EC levels, a decrease that didn't stop until age 16.

Things were quite a bit less boring when the researchers measured perspective-taking behaviors. In contrast to the EC scores, both girls and boys started out at similar levels, but they soon showed very differing trajectories. Girls' scores ramped up quickly, with especially steep increases observed between 13 and 15 years of age. Boys' scores actually went down slightly during that same period, with no measurable uptick until age 16. They never caught up, however, and at the end of the test period, their PT scores remained slightly lower than the girls'. (See Figure 7.1.)

Social Skills and Adolescence

Figure 7.1

Empathetic concern and perspective-taking skills show sex-based developmental differences in the teen brain. Highlighted below are some of the differences occurring between ages 13 and 18.

EMPATHIC CONCERN

Boys	Girls
Empathic scores (EC subscale of the IRI, see text) are lower than those of girls at age 13 and dip still lower until age 16. They rebound to previous levels by age 18.	Empathic scores are higher than those of boys at age 13 and remain constant at these higher levels through the last measure at age 18.

PERSPECTIVE TAKING

Boys	Girls
Perspective-taking scores (PT subscale of the IRI; see text) are similar to those of girls at age 13. The numbers decrease until age 16, then rise again.	Perspective-taking scores are similar to those of boys at age 13. The numbers increase between ages 13 and 15. Scores at age 18 are high than those of boys at age 18.

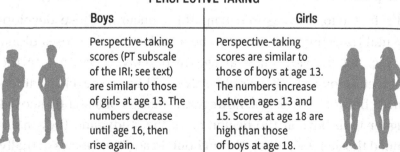

It's hardly breaking news to say adolescent girls develop faster emotionally than boys, but it's illuminating that the differences are noticeably quantifiable. In general measures of adolescent social cognition, girls are, on average, about two years ahead of boys. What happens after 18 is a subject beyond the scope of this book, though I can give a previously mentioned spoiler alert: the brains of most men and women don't finish developing until their mid-20s.

The Brains Behind the Behaviors

The neurological substrates undergirding these behaviors are slowly revealing themselves to researchers. Admittedly, it's been a tough slog. Both EC and PT neural networks are more convoluted than healthcare insurance; they involve extremely complicated networks of neurons, functionally connected and widely distributed all over the brain. Many of these networks are also involved with executive function. Two regions of the prefrontal cortex (the medial and ventromedial PFC), famously involved in impulse control, are also involved in empathy. So is the amygdala, that region mediating so many of our passions, as well as a few other exotic regions we haven't discussed, like the multitalented *superior temporal sulcus*.[20]

In adults, these networks work together in a mature, relatively coordinated fashion. In the adolescent brain, however, they're still electrical rookies. As discussed a few chapters back, most of the regions involved in executive function in teens are still getting to know each other. Since these regions also share neurological office space with EC and PT, these social behaviors are still getting acquainted, too. That means they're plastic and moldable.[21]

And that notion explains the happy outcomes behind well-designed SEL programs. The success of these programs may be due in part to the fact that the neurological substrates in teens are still forming, are still malleable and thus open to suggestion. That means there's hope for the fanboys of *Star Wars*. And even more hope for the target of their affections.

The Controversial Power of Screen Time

There are two questions I get asked a lot whenever I give a public lecture on teen brain biology. One has to do with screen time; the other has to do with bedtime. Both address "environmental" issues of how external behavioral habits affect adolescent emotional regulation. Both are voiced primarily by people born when The Beatles were still charting.

"Is the digital world making the brains of kids stupid?" (or a variation thereof) is how the screen time question is couched, and it's not usually asked with a smile. It's a good question, though. What effect—if any—does our world's growing preoccupation with screen time have on attention spans? Emotional competencies? We've spent some time discussing empathic development in a way that sounds a lot like "nature." What about the nurture side of the behavioral ledger—specifically, the digital column? (We'll address the bedtime issue in a few moments.)

Until recently, I was of two minds about the matter, and neither one wanted to deal with it. I usually hid behind a blustering grapeshot of questions: "What do you mean by 'digital'? Do you mean text messaging? Facebook? Instagram? Video games? If you mean video games, is Pong the same thing as Call of Duty? And what do you mean by 'kids'? Do you mean Generation Z? Millennials? Toddlers?" (Yes, there are apps out there targeted at babies.)

"What do you mean by 'stupid'?" I continue, "Memory erosion? Attentional state fragmentation? Corrosive social consequences? Negative changes in affect regulation?"

Besides pegging myself as a coward, you can see where I'm headed. So many variables influence this simple question that even if it weren't generationally loaded—which for many it is—this would be extremely tough to answer. Teens may have a reputation for possessing perspectives limited to 280 characters, but is that really true? Or fair?

What's not in dispute is that screen time exposure, however you describe it, is rapidly increasing. More than 70 percent of Americans (an aggregate of all ages) use social media platforms to keep up with friends and relatives.[22] Most Americans (62 percent) now get their news from Facebook alone, according to the Pew Research Center.[23] The most frequent usage of social media is by teens, of course, though it really depends upon the platform. And no wonder. More than 93 percent of all adolescents have access to the internet via some mobile device. They spend about 200 minutes a day gazing at the screens most can put in their pockets.[24] But screen time includes other formats as well as mobile devices. A study reported by the *Washington Post* found that teens spend almost nine hours a day on various social media platforms, using a variety of screens. Yep, nine *hours*.[25]

And that was in 2015.

Facts like these have nearly caused cardiac arrest in certain audiences. It's easy to distill their concerns into two issues if you listen closely, though. The first involves social interactions, especially displacement issues. They wonder if spending time online displaces spending time offline, and, if so, isn't that bad? Displacement certainly disrupts important workouts in the face-to-face interactivity gym, as well as other forms of nonverbal communication. Without such practice, the fear is that kids will become emotionally blunt instruments, developing fewer deep friendships, becoming lonelier, and losing sophisticated skills like empathizing abilities. Scattered research papers seem to reinforce the validity of that worry. One even couched the fear in psychiatric terms, saying that overexposure to two platforms, Instagram and Snapchat, powerfully (and negatively) influences a teen's mental health.[26]

Is any of that true?

You might be surprised by my answer. If you rigorously measure the use of specific social media platforms, then assay discrete behaviors with well-characterized psychometric tests, you actually *don't* find increasing social incompetence. Empathic skills, both cognitive and affective, actually *increase* with exposure to social media platforms.

Researchers in this newer generation of studies are making some truly counterintuitive findings. One tracked a group of adolescents (10–14 years of age), examining social media use over time. They wondered whether digital exposure—defined here as a mixture of usage frequency on sites like Facebook and Twitter— correlated with score changes on the AMES (Adolescent Measure of Empathy and Sympathy), a well-regarded empathy inventory. The results? Empathy scores actually improved as kids accumulated more mileage on the social media superhighway. Here's a quote from the paper: "The results showed that social media use is related to an increase in cognitive and affective empathy over time. Specifically, adolescents' social media use improved both their ability to understand (cognitive empathy) and share the feelings of their peers (affective empathy)."[27]

Believe it or not, things get better with screens.

Why? The researchers, underscoring a need for replication, are hesitant to speculate. It's known that social media elevates a person's feelings of closeness to their friends (peer attachment), something also correlated with empathy. Being able to keep track of a person's life circumstances over time increases the potential for greater understanding and emotional sharing, too.

But all that is simple speculation. At this point, researchers are still fielding responses like "Really?" and "You've got to be kidding." It's another great example about why you have to do the research, especially when facts have to compete with opinions for intellectual oxygen.

That answers a question about empathy, but what about other selections in the social cognition buffet? Are there social abilities that actually get hurt by the digital world? The real answer is that no one knows—the medium is still too new—but hints exist that social media isn't a blanket enhancer of social skills. Consider, for example, that research on the ability of a teen to decode nonverbal information in real time via flesh-and-blood social interactions suggests that digital natives aren't as competent as prior generations.

That hypothesis sets the stage for a mildly mean pre/post experiment. What if you took away adolescent screen time for a while? Would those skills suddenly rebound? The results of one clever experiment out of UCLA tested a group of 6th graders. It's one of the few times when the entire experiment, from design to results, is revealed in the title: "Five Days at Outdoor Education Camp Without Screens Improves Preteen Skills with Nonverbal Emotion Cues."

That's right: researchers gave these 6th grade adolescents a camping experience *sans* electronics as part of a pre/post experimental design employing industry-standard psychometric tests. These included a facial decoding skills test (the CASP—Child and Adolescent Scale of Participation) and a general nonverbal cue competency test (the DANVA2—Diagnostic Assessment of Nonverbal Accuracy). In line with people who think screen time should come with some kind of warning label, here's how the authors described their findings: "After five days interacting face-to-face without the use of any screen-based media, preteen's recognition of nonverbal emotion cues improved significantly more than that of the control group."[28]

What should we make of this? The early returns on this subject suggest the effects of social media are complex, which is another way of saying the final answer is going to be uneven. Social media use improves skills like empathy while simultaneously degrading the nonverbal interpretation toolkit. Since nonverbal interpretation skills are thought to be important players on Team Emotional Competence, that's a real head-scratcher.

Fortunately, we don't have to wait for these research kinks to be worked out to have some practical things to say about SEL programs. Whichever way the dust settles, it suggests that the best SEL programs—to be deployed in earnest in the Better School for the Teen Brain—will both incorporate the strengths of screen time and fill in the deficits screen time creates. I'll have more to say about this shortly.

Right now, I want address the other cluster of questions I get asked a lot, which have to do with sleep. The issue usually comes down to a verbal skirmish occurring between parents of teens and school districts about what time the school day should begin. But, as you'll see, it also has a lot to do with executive function, especially EF's emotional regulation side.

Sleep and Beyond

Some families would rather undergo a purely recreational colonoscopy than engage in the struggle to awaken their teenage kids in time for school. Our own family wrestled with this. It could take a medal-worthy act of courage to coax our ever-drowsy eldest son Joshua to get up and preserve his attendance record.

A cottage industry has sprung up with solutions for families with sleepy teens like ours,[29] and we became experts in the business. We found some of the funniest, most creative solutions came in the design of alarm clocks. One machine, christened Clocky, is a device sporting two giant wheels and a motor. When the alarm goes off, it starts driving around the bedroom; you have to chase it to turn it off, which of course means you have to get out of bed, which is the point. Two devices we found involved money. The first is something you connect to your bank account. Unless you get up and turn the alarm off within a designated window, it will automatically donate funds to an organization you despise. The second, simplicity itself, includes a shredder into which you load paper money (the ad shows a $100 bill). Failure to turn the alarm off within the allotted time transforms your money into confetti.

Eventually Josh—and we—found a routine that worked. But our son is hardly alone in the daily cage match to get his teen brain to school. Why do adolescents have so much time-based toil and trouble?

There are a few reasons. Not only do they need a five-scoops helping of sleep—they need to experience sleep at specific times.[30] A joint study between Oxford and Harvard calculated what ideal start times for school would look like if teen cognitive optimization were the driving goal. Their recommendations surprised most people. In the ideal world, classes would start at 8:30 for 10-year-olds, 10:00 for 16-year-olds, and 11:00 for 18-year-olds.[31]

These recommendations run over the typical American school schedule like a circadian Sherman's march to the sea. Implementing such radical changes is costly to districts, costly to extracurricular sports programs, and costly to impossibly busy parental work schedules.

Even so, a number of school districts have negotiated an armistice with these data, switching to later start times (8:30 a.m. is common). The cognitive consequences of even this modest change have been studied, famously at the University of Minnesota (a study involving more than 9,000 high schoolers). A teaching guide found online summarized the findings: "Grades, tests scores, and overall performance in core subjects advanced significantly when school start times were switched to later hours."[32]

These benefits were like behavioral free money. They included reduction in tardiness, truancy, and dropout rates. Later-starting teens exhibited increased executive function (measured by focusing behaviors) and improvements in mood. It's that last behavior that links directly with our discussion of SEL curricula. Even the best programs in the world lose effectiveness if they have to teach sleep-deprived, cranky-as-Model-Ts teens. Addressing students who have acquired the proper amount of sleep gives such classes their best shot at performing as advertised.[33]

There's an additional benefit, related not to brains but to spreadsheets. Switching to later times actually makes long-term financial sense. The necessary changes to school infrastructure and to sports and bus schedules might be costly in the short term, but according to the Rand Corporation, a statewide, universal shift to an 8:30 start time would result in "economic gains" that amount to $8.6 billion after just 2 years and an astonishing $83 billion after 10 years.[34]

Designing a Better School for the Teen Brain

This tug-of-war with data is more evidence that middle and high school schedules were never created with the teen brain in mind—and even more proof that they should be. As we continue our fantasy about the secondary school of the future, we take both SEL programs and the receptivity of adolescents to their content seriously. And like all the other suggestions in this book, we design the programs to aid in teens' developing executive function.

The first step is to make SEL programs a regular, nonoptional feature of a teen's curricular feeding schedule. Selecting the best programs, using the SAFE recommendations mentioned earlier, is probably the first order of business. Taking into account that social media might actually aid and abet SEL skills, such programs could be tested with the insertion of a digital component (whether it's effective or not would be a research issue). Implementing an SEL program represents not only a chance to aid teen development, but also an opportunity to investigate some behavioral science questions, perhaps in collaboration with an existing college of education.

Maximizing the success of SEL programs benefits from optimizing the environment for the teen brain, of course. That includes addressing ideal teen sleep schedules, which means swallowing the unpleasant pill of start time issues. My fantasy school conforms to the recommendations of the Harvard/Oxford findings. This recommendation intersects with executive function twice: once for a teen's sleep debt, the other for preparation for SEL programs—and, really, every other class.

Like prior Better School for the Teen Brain recommendations, these suggestions focus directly on teenagers, rather than their parents or teachers. And the focus is admittedly personal, addressing lifestyle issues from their beds to their cell phones. I'm not done, however; there's one more personal issue to address.

When mentioning the effects of screen time, you might recall I was responding to questions I regularly get from the audiences to whom I speak. My response to screen time and socialization is positive, but that's hardly the only category about which I get asked. Another common question has to do with attentional states: "Is screen time changing my 13-year-old's attention span?"

Here the story isn't so surprising, or positive. As we'll see in the next chapter, screen time is not 100 percent beneficent (although as we'll also see, there is a workaround). We'll begin with a discussion of the last movie I'll mention in this book, one of my family's favorites.

8

SCREEN TIME MEETS MINDFULNESS TRAINING

Our last chapter—and final design impetus for the Better School for the Teen Brain—concerns an odd hybrid of adolescent behavior and meditation. I've seen one of the finest examples of its behavioral effects in an unexpected place: *Fantastic Mr. Fox,* a stop-action film directed by Wes Anderson.

If you haven't seen this tasty morsel of a flick, based on the Roald Dahl book of the same name, I recommend it highly. It's about a family of sentient, English-speaking foxes living in the British countryside. A side plot of the movie involves two adolescent foxes.

The first is the son of the protagonist, a ginger-colored fox named Ash. The second is Ash's cousin, a pale-gray fox named Kristofferson. Kristofferson's father is quite ill, and the boy has been sent to live with Ash and family until Dad gets better (if he gets better). There's immediate relational conflict between the two kids, for twitchy, self-conscious Ash has a chip the size of London on his shoulder. As the movie soon reveals, Ash is all too aware that he's not good at much of anything. And what makes it even worse for him is that Cousin Kristofferson is good at everything.

And I do mean everything. Kristofferson's good at diving, karate, a sport called "whack-bat," and getting a girlfriend. He's even good at being emotionally centered, due to his regular meditation practice. That's where his story enters into this book. Meditation is a lifestyle with this guy.

In one scene, Ash's dad (the titular Mr. Fox) gets injured. The boy is relieved that his dad's debilitation is not as serious as his uncle's illness. Kristofferson's dad, Ash notes, has "one foot in the grave and three feet on a banana peel." Kristofferson is naturally hurt and disturbed by his cousin's words, but he deals with his frustration in an extraordinary way: by announcing he's going to go meditate for a half hour. Illustrating that there's a difference between acceptance and forgiveness, however, Kristofferson also tells Ash he has 29 minutes to think about how to apologize.[1]

Kristofferson is using meditation like some people use alcohol, only without the side effects. It's a lifestyle, a social lubricant, and a stress reducer. I couldn't believe I was actually watching it applied by a teen character in an animated movie. But I was. And I was struck by the potential that mindfulness training has for building executive function. In this chapter, we're going to explore Kristofferson's perspective and consider the role mindfulness might play in the school of the future. Because mindfulness is all about finding calm and order amid apparent chaos, it's a fitting wrap-up of our discussion about how best to educate the teenaged brain.

We Start with Anxiety

Environmental pressure can drive adolescents into a wall of anxiety, actually approaching—and in some cases exceeding—the stress their parents typically experience. A report published by the American Psychological Association (APA) quantified this stress, using a standard 10-point stress scale. Adult figures crossed the finish line at a stout 5.1, teens at 5.8. By contrast, the number where most teens feel emotionally healthy is around 3.9.

These results are evidenced by their glass-half-empty feelings about their lives. About a third of teens described being overwhelmed, and a third felt their stress had increased from the year before. Only 16 percent described a decrease. More than double that figure (34 percent) felt that things were going to get worse *next* year.[2]

At one level, teen angst is as normal as their proclivity for chicken strips. Moodiness and emotional intensity are the hallmarks of mainstream teen behavior, after all, and the APA data primarily rely on self-reporting.

Still, all is not well. Typical adolescent experience is now powerful enough to move the stress needle from "discomfort" to "in need of psychiatric attention." And that's decidedly not typical. According to the National Institute of Mental Health, about 6.3 million American adolescents (approximately 25 percent of all teens, more of them girls than boys) suffer from an anxiety disorder. That's an increase since 2012.[3]

This uptick is as puzzling as a sudden tantrum, and for two reasons. The first is that, in the years before 2012, the rates of teenage anxiety had been more or less flat, with no real increase observable. The second may give a clue to the first: anxiety has somehow become an equal opportunity offender, touching a wide adolescent demographic. Increases were seen from city kids to farm kids, from teens who don't plan on attending college to teens who do.

These puzzling observations aren't reassuring, obviously— and they're made worse by evidence suggesting this prevalence is woefully underreported. It's estimated that only one in five kids who struggle with anxiety receives therapy.[4] Many teens, apparently, just live with the disorder. Maybe they don't even recognize it as a disorder.

Why is all this is happening? The question is tough to answer. As with most human behaviors stretched out over diverse populations, causal reasons are complex and elusive. Parents play a role, either through being thoroughly overbearing or being willfully neglectful. Economics is a factor, too. Today's teens were elementary students when their families were digging their way out of the dark financial hole of the Great Recession. Stressed-out parents often produce stressed-out kids.

The largest factor, however, may not involve parents or their fiscal solvency. It may involve the current, hyper-input-driven lifestyle of today's teenager. Janis Whitlock, a researcher who studies teen anxiety at Cornell University, certainly thinks so. She feels the biggest factor is the overwhelming amount of stimulation teenagers experience on a moment-to-moment basis. In a *Time* magazine interview, Whitlock said of teens, "If you wanted to create an environment to churn out really angsty people, we've done it. . . . It's that they're in a cauldron of stimulus they can't get away from, or don't want to get away from, or don't know how to get away from."[5]

If overstimulation is the largest issue, then decreasing the constancy of input might go a long way toward turning down the anxiety volume knob. But this isn't an easy sell. The noisy digital world defining most teenagers today—and many adults, for that matter—isn't filled with long stretches of calming walks in Zen gardens.

Do we have to change the channel on our thinking? Figuring out how the digital world relates to the cognitive toxicology at which Dr. Whitlock is taking aim is where we are headed next. For better or for worse, the data are trending in a particular direction, and interestingly, the whole thing relates to executive function. We begin with one of the saddest websites I have ever visited.

The Attentional Spotlight

As far as conversation goes, this text string doesn't sound all that interesting. The author, Alexander Heat, a student at University of Northern Colorado, was responding to a friend's text:

> FRIEND: Hey man I had to run out for like an hour

> ALEX: Sounds good my man, sea soon, ill two[6]

This exchange is compelling for a tragic reason: it includes Alex's last words. He was texting while driving. While typing a message he would never complete, his car drifted into the wrong lane, then careened down a steep hill. Alex died in the hospital. His parents published these texts in the hometown paper as a warning against texting and driving. I'm recounting this experience in the same spirit.

Alex died because of a peculiar characteristic of human cognition, a property belonging to something called the *attentional spotlight*. Originating from vision research, this cognitive gadget allows you to focus on a specific stimulus. It's active now, even as you're reading these words. It can only focus on one thing at a time, unfortunately, which is why you can't simultaneously read this page and the one right next to it. That characteristic is what killed Alex. When his mind focused on texting, he couldn't focus on driving.

As we've discussed, focusing behavior is a card-carrying member of Club Executive Function. Focusing is usually measured by subjects concentrating on something, then suddenly experiencing some inconvenient interruption. Scientists measure how long it takes to recover focus. This skill is obviously important for functioning at home and school, or any activity related to getting ahead in a knowledge-based economy, and it's surprisingly fragile. People who are stressed, anxious, depressed, or just sleepy often find they can't focus on anything. From schoolwork to job-work, the care and feeding of focusing behavior is obviously very important.

With attention as our chaperone, we're going to plunge back headlong into Whitlock's "cauldron of stimulus" quote, necessarily reengaging in the digital debate outlined in the last chapter. Our subject won't be relational/emotional executive function, however. Instead, we're going to pole-vault to the other side of EF— cognitive control—and discuss spotlight issues. I will outline the debate, explain a disturbing trend line, then return to Whitlock.

More Controversy

The squabbles concerning teens and the digital world are currently active—and messy, as we've discussed. Some think the screen-soaked world is cognitively nutritious. Others think the digital world is as healthy as a corn dog. Remembering that teens spend inordinate amounts of time looking at screens (nine hours a day!), we all can agree the issue isn't trivial.

What does the literature say about people who sluice their minds with video games and cell phones and text messages? To understand research findings, we have first got to cover some key definitions.

Attentional states come in two flavors, *focused attention* and *distributed attention*. Focused attention is just what it sounds like. Distributed attention is what allows you to process information at the 40,000-foot level.[7] What experiments researchers perform depends upon what attentional type they want to measure.

Considering what species of screen time you're stretching out on the exam table is also important. Does texting incessantly strain the same cognitive resources as bingeing on Call of Duty? Is playing electronic chess different from playing Mario Kart, and are all these different from checking your Facebook newsfeed hourly? Historically, there's been a lot of emphasis on video game exposure, perhaps because it was so much easier to measure. We'll also focus on video games, but I'm most concerned with screen time, the common digital ingredient that involves stimuli capable of dazzling teen eyes at flash rates faster than what their real worlds normally offer.

Good News and Bad News

What the research literature says about attentional states and screen time (defined broadly) is frustrating enough to make you want to trash your reading glasses. Researchers draw two general conclusions, and they're almost completely contradictory. We'll start with data on the advocacy side of the street.

Consider this quote from a *Scientific American* article on the brain-boosting power of video games: "[Video games] have now become tools in research facilities because of their ability to enhance attention."[8]

Yes, they used the word "enhance." The claim is that digital fantasy worlds create fantastic gymnasiums for exercising mental focus. Players must constantly shift between fast-moving scenarios that require sophisticated problem solving. Solutions build cumulatively, usually in pursuit of a larger, steadily present goal. Many cognitive processes improve upon increased exposure to such screen time, from faster information processing to improved visuospatial skills. Even impulse control gets into the act. Many games require *hours* of repetition to solve, with one false move pushing you back to square 1. You must tolerate a fair amount of annoyance if you want to continue playing.

Researchers have even tackled adults' greatest concern regarding teens and their Xboxes: what does persistent exposure to video games do to academic performance in adolescents? Research results can be found in the title of one published finding: "Video Games Do Not Negatively Impact Adolescent Academic Performance."[9]

Screen time seems to help the brain. Screen time doesn't seem to hurt the GPA. Nothing to see here, folks. Perhaps we should move along.

The Dark Side

Not so fast, say other researchers. They point to other findings that demonstrate the *exact opposite thing*. One study from Iowa State used a Swiss Army knife collection of EF tests on kids and found whopping differences between heavy-use gamers and light-use enthusiasts. Extended screen time had a negative impact on something called *proactive cognitive control,* the neural gizmo that permits you to stay focused when attending to a lecture or studying on your own. The press release from the university says it all: "Iowa State study finds high volume video gamers have more difficulty staying attentive."[10] The contrast between the two positions might as well be a tutorial on the definition of "antonym."

While these two camps are still battling for supremacy, one appears to be gaining strength, in part because of something almost completely bereft of statistical opinion: brain-imaging studies. Research seems to demonstrate that excessive exposure to Kingdom Screen Time acts the same way excess ocean acts against a limestone cliff: it erodes and changes the neural landscape, reducing the thickness of the orbitofrontal cortex in males (frontal lobe) and rewiring dopamine-rich pleasure regions in their limbic systems. Psychiatrists believe some of their younger patients have essentially become addicted to their screens, and one has christened it Electronic Screen Syndrome. Behavioral characteristics include impulsiveness, moodiness, and an inability to pay attention. The title of the article describing this perspective says it all: "Gray Matters: Too Much Screen Time Damages the Brain."[11]

So which is it, folks? Is screen time a brain-empowering bottle of vitamins or cognition-clogging fast food? Does the digital world help or hurt attentional states?

Whenever I see two points of view this polarizing, I usually just shrug off the confusion by saying we don't know enough. The implication is that more work needs to be done. That's all still true here, orbitofrontals notwithstanding. The problem is, professionals other than psychiatrists and brain imagers have taken up the offer to do that work, and clear trend lines are forming. The data's arc looks like it's bending toward the negative, suggesting that Whitlock may be onto something with her proclamations connecting stimuli and teen anxiety.

In support of this glass-half-empty perspective, one important experiment that's received a lot of press (and engendered some controversy) came directly from the entrails of the digital beast: Palo Alto, California. These were the experiments of Eyal Ophir, Clifford Nass, and Anthony Wagner from Stanford University.

The research inspiration began with one obvious and one not-so-obvious and therefore surprising observation. It concerned the screen time habits of Stanford undergraduates, who had probably picked up those habits as high schoolers. Some kids fit the classic definition of the digital native: lots of windows open on their laptops; simultaneous media usage; and tons of switching between phones, computer games, and videos. The scientists called them HMMs (heavy media multitaskers). The surprise came from the fact that there were other kids of the same generation who didn't behave anything like this. Their screen time world had little simultaneous usage and less task switching. The scientists called them LMMs (light media multitaskers).

The researchers asked nosy questions of these digitally indigenous populations, mostly related to their distractibility, concentration, and focus—all hallmarks of EF. Both groups were given "filtering tasks," measuring how well they dealt with distractions and task switching in order to arrive at some correct test answer. The hypothesis was that the HMMs, who were champions at this sort of thing, would zip through these filtering tasks, giving correct responses in record time. The LMMs, decidedly not seasoned multitaskers, would poke along and take longer to get the right answers.

The results show the need for putting in time at the lab bench. The exact *opposite* of the hypothesis was observed. HMMs had poorer performance on the tasks, were more susceptible to distractions, had poorer short-term memory, and took longer to get the correct responses. On average, LMMs only needed about 323 milliseconds to get the right answer; it took HMMs 400 milliseconds or longer. No matter how many times they did variations on these tests, the same counterintuitive finding was obtained.[12] Ophir said of the HMMs in an interview, "The high multitaskers are always drawing from all the information in front of them. They can't keep things separate in their minds." Nass was no less abrasive: "They're suckers for irrelevancy. Everything distracts them."[13]

This isn't a one-off situation. Other researchers, behaviorists like Iowa State's Craig Anderson, have found similar attention-eroding effects with heavy screen time (and even associations with aggressive behavior, which is a whole other can of worms). Like I said, the arc is bending toward there being negative effects of screen time. And that implies that something should be done. Does the peer-reviewed world provide solutions as well as indictments?

Indeed it does, and in a most delightful way. The secret involves Japanese gardens.

The Genius of Peace

I admit to being a sucker for Japanese gardens, and I lay the blame squarely on my childhood. I was an Air Force brat born in Tachikawa Air Force Base, a now-defunct installation just west of Tokyo. My early life was filled with plant-based Japanese artistic idioms. My hometown of Seattle has a beautiful Japanese garden that I visit regularly. There are flowing streams, beautiful bridges, and enough koi to fill several pet stores. Whenever I visit that garden, I turn off my cell phone. For the next hour, I feel calm, collected, visually enchanted, and time-warped back to my preschool years. I always regret having to turn my chatty electronic ADHD-afflicted device back on when I leave these gardens.

There may be a powerful reason for this calm-and-regret spin cycle. Being able to watch koi swim in a lyrical, simple space is a reminder of the power of the present. The phone is a reminder of things I have yet to do.

Researchers like Jon Kabat-Zinn and Ellen Langer have tapped into this power of the present, and they didn't need a Japanese garden to do it. These godparents of so-called mindfulness training found ways to capture the power of being present, gift-wrapping their ideas in behavioral protocols that have changed the life of millions. They also had the guts to research why it was so powerful and, in so doing, awarded a good idea with a solid peer-reviewed merit badge. We're now going to explore the concept, focusing its powerful lens on the frothing cauldron of the teenaged brain. Let's begin with definitions.

The Power of Mindfulness

At its core, mindfulness is a form of mental training, but it's like a boot camp run by your best friend. Though a number of different training procedures have been published, they share common elements. One is *object focus,* learning to concentrate on a single object for an extended period. For some reason, raisins are popular. By concentrating on the shriveled grape, you begin to notice things about its features that you previously had no time to contemplate. Another exercise is *body awareness,* such as engaging in a "body scan," where you focus in a linear, graduated fashion on various body parts (like the back of your head or your ankles). A final common element may be the most important, at least from a neuroscientific perspective. It concerns *focused breathing.* Mindfulness teaches you to breathe in and out slowly, paying attention to each inhale and exhale.

Researchers have been studying a specific dialect of mindfulness for many years, cheerfully turning its foundational ideas into data points as reproducible as rabbits.[14] The benefits appear to come from the close interaction of three components—think of it as the trinity—two of which are members in good standing of Team Executive Function.

The first component is related to boosting *attentional control.* When you focus on a specific, emotionally neutral subject (something like a raisin or the tip of your nose), your brain can't simultaneously focus on other things that bother you. It's one of the plus sides to your spotlight's inability to multitask. With practice, you train your brain not to stray from the target under consideration. Even if you go off course, mindfulness tells you it's all right, then entreats you to gently return to your focusing exercise.

The second component of mindfulness is *emotional regulation,* wherein mindfulness tries to put a restraining order against your toxic, out-of-control feelings. Formally defined, emotional regulation describes approaches people use to control how their feelings are experienced. These strategies run the gamut from selecting which emotions should be recruited for further processing to the length of time they're allowed to hang around. Mindfulness boosts this regulatory skill—yes, it's a skill—which may partially be a result of the behavioral ecology that mindfulness practice encourages you to enter. Mindfulness places a strong emphasis on cultivating nonjudgmental attitudes. During the meditation, mindfulness asks you to consider the events and experiences in your life without evaluating them. The word "should" is replaced by the word "accept." Mindfulness does not take away the icky parts of life, but it provides the subject a way of looking at them through gentler eyes. Without the taxing energy of future obligation, emotions have a cleaner shot at being regulated. Eventually, people learn to surround such nonjudgmental ecology with personal warmth, even compassion.

The final component is called *altered self-awareness,* a form of anti-narcissism. The idea is that by focusing on a raisin, you're not focusing on yourself. By focusing on your toes, you're not focusing on how many people have wronged you. Mindfulness trains people to diminish recursive self-referential habits by temporarily focusing on something other than what they are the center of. This focal offshoring is related to the attentional training of the first component. The nonjudgmental characteristic also serves as a cognitive anesthetic, making it easier to do.

Adventures in Driving

By way of full disclosure, I will state that I am an active practitioner of mindfulness. Probably the gold standard for those who wish to learn about mindfulness at home—as I did—is an eight-week course found in *The Mindful Way Workbook* by John Teasdale, Mark Williams, and Zindel Segal.[15] There are also plenty of apps and computer-based programs on mindfulness, but here I need to roll out the *caveat emptor* artillery: care must be taken to ensure that alternative mindfulness training methods have been tested as rigorously as the one I just mentioned. To get the research benefits, you have to emulate the research protocols.

I'd like to illustrate how mindfulness can change people's reactions with a personal example.

I was driving on one of Seattle's crowded freeways at rush hour—an experience as fun-filled as a colonoscopy—when what appeared to be a teenage driver suddenly cut in front of me. I had to slam on the brakes to keep from hitting him, and it flashed through my mind that I might be the unhappy initiator of a chain of whiplash-inducing, lawsuit-bringing rear-end collisions. Fortunately, the guy behind me was following far enough back that nothing was triggered except my active imagination.

Normally this near-wreck would infuriate me, regardless of the driver's age, and my autonomic nervous system would start preflighting my body for fight-or-flight operations. What happened this time was that I thought about the top of my head, which is often the first step in a mindfulness body scan. "How did *a mindfulness cue* just elbow its way into my driving behavior?" I thought, amazed. Then I felt my diaphragm obediently disobeying its sympathetic marching orders. I began breathing more deliberately and deeply. I wasn't rejecting my angry feelings—I could still sense them—but now they didn't seem to matter. The training was becoming reflexive, and I couldn't have been happier.

Researchers are beginning to understand that, with consistent practice, anyone can develop this mindfulness-triggering reflex, even grizzled neuroscientists on their way to work. And it's not just good for daily living. In adults, mindfulness-based interventions (MBIs) can successfully treat a wide variety of mood disorders. When combined with another three-letter therapy protocol, cognitive behavioral therapy (CBT), mindfulness incites some of the best treatment outcomes for depression and anxiety that exist.[16]

Unexpectedly, the data embrace more than just mood disorders. Mindfulness aids in reducing chronic pain, cigarette addiction, and even irritable bowel syndrome.[17] It's no wonder that many American institutions, from the military to professional sports organizations, are all widely adopting the practice.

Should American middle and high schools adopt the practice with similar vigor? Remembering that teen brains are nothing like adult versions, it's a valid question.

The answer is an enthusiastic yes, even for those kids just starting puberty.[18] One particularly thorough study done in 489 adolescents, examining both middle and high school students, serves as an example of this growing mountain of really good news.

A Randomized Trial with Teens

In this study, following standard practice for causal work, students were randomly assigned into two groups, treatment and control groups. The treatment group received six weeks of integrative body-mind training (IBMT) for 30 minutes a day.

The end results for this group were a stunner, with great tidings visible at both the cognitive control and the emotional regulation piers of the executive function bridge. In the treatment group, gains were observed in selective attention tasks, sustained attention tasks, and Raven's Matrices scores (a measure of nonverbal abstract reasoning). The teens' grades also quantifiably improved in three areas: mathematics, literacy, and second-language proficiency. Emotional boosts included improved social interactions and the overall presence of positive emotions.[19] Try getting exposure to Grand Theft Auto to do that for you!

What is the procedure for conjuring up this behavioral fairy dust? Though many protocols exist, they tend to follow a specific pattern, with the best ones administered by a certified instructor. Here's how the daily 30-minute IBMT worked:

1. *Pre-session warm-up* (5 minutes)—A transition stage. The coach prepped students for the main event, providing directions and setting environmental conditions designed to bring them into the proper frame of mind. This is no easy feat for this age group, which is why you need a good coach.

2. *Practice session* (20 minutes)—The main event. There was the standard mixture of object focus, body scans, and other exercises, guided by instructions on a CD. The coach monitored the students as they eased into their meditation stances. Struggling kids received either immediate feedback or comments after the session was completed.

3. *Post-session cooldown* (5 minutes)—Group discussion. The coach essentially "took the temperature" of the class, using that feedback to ensure the group got the most out of the session.

The Brains Behind Mindfulness

These steps might sound simple—indeed, they are—but a mindfulness habit can be tough to form in a world whose cultural gears seem stuck in permanent overdrive. Simple is not the same thing as easy.

It's easy to be distracted when your life seems caught in a perpetual spin cycle. The rewards of removing yourself from the chaos, however, are huge. Statistically, if you make mindfulness as much a habit as checking your text messages, you'll see real positive behavioral changes. These alterations can even be observed neuroanatomically. Mindfulness does a victory lap around your life by literally changing your brain structure.

But first you must form the habit, and that's *not* easy. Recently I got a reminder of all the obstacles we face. I'd been asked to give a guest lecture on memory and attention at a local high school, and on the way there, I stopped off at a neighborhood coffee shop for my afternoon infusion of Seattle's version of vitamin C (caffeine). The young barista appeared to be alone behind the counter, and she was trying to juggle five or so beverage orders, warm a sandwich in an oven (the "ready" ringer kept braying as loud as a donkey), and navigate the cash register, all while straining to keep a smile on her face. The line of customers kept growing. This was life in a pressure cooker.

Once I got my coffee, I entered the school and sat down in the classroom where I would be giving my talk. The high school students came trundling in. Most were texting something on their mobile devices; some had laptops open. Many were wearing headphones. All seemed to be juggling a hundred things at once, just like the barista. On the teacher's desk was a coffee mug emblazoned with a saying that seemed to explain everything—the barista, the students, and maybe even the teacher: "My brain has too many tabs open."

Perfect, I thought.

To understand what mindfulness does to the brain, we need to review the concept of functional connectivity. We discussed previously that brain regions are composed of myriads of neurons biologically soldered together to form networks. Cognitive processes begin to function when these networks are stimulated in specific ways. The whole concept is called *functional connectivity,* defined informally as networks activated together to provide some function. Executive function is a perfect example of neural networks firing in specific patterns to create its various behaviors.

When mindfulness is practiced with the consistency of a mortgage payment, the functional connectivity between certain brain regions begins to change. Even the regions themselves are altered. We know, for example, that the amygdalae, those almond-shaped structures that supervise experiences like fear, start to lose weight (they actually shrink). This, in turn, weakens many of their functional connections to other regions of the brain.

At the same time these fear centers are deactivating, regions involved in our ability to attend to specific stimuli begin to strengthen. This occurs most noticeably in the prefrontal cortex, which gets thicker. As we've discussed many times, the PFC is involved in attention and concentration, so this fact may not be all that surprising. But this might be: the more you do reps in the mindfulness gym, the greater (and more stable) these changes become. That's why you have to make it a habit.

Interestingly, not all functional connections involving the PFC get stronger. Connections that rope the PFC to a region called the *anterior cingulate cortex* (ACC) begin to weaken with increased mindfulness. In fact, they become uncoupled. That's an important change, and a very good thing for most people. The ACC is directly involved in feeling the subjective ickiness of pain.[20]

Learning to focus is greatly aided by the signature dish in the mindfulness menu: conscious breathing. It's been known for years that consciously controlled respiration has a profound impact on stress, arousal states, and certain emotions. Recent research suggests a reason. There's a small region in your brain named the *locus coeruleus* that is involved in influencing your arousal states (like panic). It's the principal site of the brain's manufacture of the stress hormone *norepinephrine*. We now know, at least in mice, that this region also collects information about how breathing is going. It uses this information to both manufacture and regulate arousal. Regular deep breathing may assist calming behaviors by modulating stress hormone manufacture in the locus coeruleus—all done on the back of these connections.[21]

This is science in the fun zone. Taken together, a remarkably detailed neurological picture is emerging about why mindfulness can be so powerful. It's changing the way the brain looks at fear and pain while at the same time strengthening regions associated with controlling them. The neural substrates that mediate executive function are being rewired, all because you've decided to concentrate on the lovely contours of your earlobe.

Most of the work mentioned here, however, was not done in populations where impulsivity can turn to crazy in a nanosecond. Instead, it was done with adults (primarily college undergraduates). Do the mechanisms that work so well in adults also work in our favorite age group?

The answer is disappointing: we just don't know. We think they do—there are small hints—but the data just aren't strong enough to make it settled law. A quote from a paper authored by a pair of researchers in the United Kingdom—both doubtful and hopeful—illustrates the current state of research: "It is possible that mindfulness practice could encourage connections between the relevant prefrontal structures in adolescents, stabilizing arousal and reducing harmful risk-taking."[22]

We don't have to wait for the data about neurological underpinnings to catch up before we make practical suggestions, fortunately. The behavioral data are muscular enough to responsibly inform the design of our school of the future.

Designing a Better School for the Teen Brain

In my imaginary secondary school of the future, mindfulness is as regular a part of a teen's daily experiences as Snapchat. This mindfulness fantasy has curriculum, teacher, student, and physical room components (see Figure 8.1), and making it a reality involves a four-step process.

The first step is selecting the curriculum to be studied. There is a growing list of materials aimed at the education market. How do you separate the wheat from the chaff? How do you know which programs might fit best in your situation?

Integrating Mindfulness

Figure 8.1

In the Better School for the Teen Brain, mindfulness exercises are as regular a part of the curriculum as language arts. Here's how any school might pursue this goal.

1 **Selection**
A committee selects the mindfulness training curriculum that best suits the students and the school.

2 **Certification**
Designated faculty receive training to become certified in mindfulness techniques; these instructors go on to train other faculty and staff.

3 **Classroom Creation**
The school sets up a mindfulness classroom for the certified instructors, faculty, staff, and students to use for mindfulness training and practice.

4 **Repeated Exposure**
Instructors teach a mindfulness course to incoming students. Students begin each school day with a 15- to 30-minute mindfulness exercise supervised by trained faculty.

Fortunately, a lot of the curating has already been done. A team of researchers from the United States, Canada, and the United Kingdom has sifted through the thicket of programs, and they put their recommendations in a paper titled "Integrating Mindfulness Training into K–12 Education: Fostering the Resilience of Teachers and Students."[23]

Since the best-tested programs are administered by certified instructors, the second step is for teachers to obtain that certification. Certification can be awarded in many places, some online, some in bricks-and-mortar institutions.[24] Ideally, these designated experts would be recruited from existing faculty, counseling staff, or both. Once certified, instructors could take the entire school administration and teachers on a retreat to teach them the basics in preparation for the school year.

The third step is creating a "mindfulness classroom," a physical location where this curriculum can be taught. In my fantasy, the space is a double-roomed area where the multiweek training could be taught continuously, and where students and staff could go for midday mindfulness breaks. No screens *of any kind* would be allowed. The room would be fitted with an audio system, flooded with green light, and fairly laughing with plants.

There's a reason for that color requirement. Research originally done at the University of Michigan and the University of Illinois found that the color green helps students focus. That's green in the visible light spectrum, good old 510 nanometers and its close electromagnetic relatives. The effect was even dose-dependent. On typical tests of attention, the greener the room, the higher the score. The boost was especially pronounced if that wavelength came from natural settings, like trees and plants. The effect was so strong it even relieved certain symptoms in students with ADD. Conclusions from one paper found that "children function better than usual after activities in green settings, and that the 'greener' a child's play area, the less severe his or her attention deficit symptoms."[25]

That's quite a statement to make, and, for our purposes, we should approach it with caution. While these effects have been well studied in children, adolescents have not yet been targeted. That turns this suggestion into another research project—and provides another to create a double classroom so that the second space could serve as a control where lighting, plants, and even the auditory space can be manipulated. These ongoing research projects would ferret out under what environmental conditions teens' executive function skills thrived.

The fourth and final step is to involve the students. Instructors would teach mindfulness practice—the well-researched six- to eight-week course—to bring each student up to speed for the rest of year. The course could then be offered each fall for incoming freshmen, and even throughout the year. Once proficient at mindfulness practice, the teens would start the day in a somewhat redesigned homeroom period that sets the last 15 minutes aside for a grounding session.

I realize many of the ideas in this chapter and in this book—including the odd ducks like dedicated, green-hued mindfulness classrooms—represent a radical departure from current education practice. Most middle and high schools were not designed with the adolescent brain in mind, let alone with a specific focus on the development of executive function. Yet, as these pages describe, boosting EF predicts academic and social successes in almost every way you can measure them. These data clamber up onto their soapboxes and preach to anyone who'll listen. Green rooms are a part of it, as is exercise, SEL coursework, and teaching adults how to parent their kids. Education really is in the business of brain development, and everything we do in secondary education should consider teen brain development and the various ways we might better support teenagers' cognitive and social-emotional growth and well-being.

I am sympathetic to the fact that change is hard even when everyone agrees with facts that support change, and it's even harder when such agreement does not exist. Unfortunately, ambiguity characterizes many of the fragile sinews linking the science of learning to the practice of learning. That's why more than a few of the suggestions I have are really research projects aimed at *discovering* best practices. Implementation would come only when these ideas have been discovered to work.

I'm happy to embrace such difficulty, order another round of experiments, then call it a day. Ambiguity is actually part and parcel of the scientific enterprise, a real sign you've bellied up to the boundary between the known and the unknown. Given the importance of understanding the weird and wonderful world of the adolescent learner in the light of current progress, it's the best place we can be.

Epilogue:
Building That Bridge

I started this book describing Evel Knievel's outlandish effort to cross the Snake River Canyon using what amounted to a two-wheeled rocket ship.

I likened his attempt, and the famous gorge that defeated him, to a gap in the U.S. education system. Though our elementary schools are competitive internationally, and our higher education systems are the envy of the world, we fail badly at traversing the canyon-sized achievement gap between the two levels. Our middle and high schools, the realm of the still-under-construction teenaged brain, are falling short. As a brain scientist, I used this book to explore the question of how best to span that gap.

A quick solution might be to create the curricular equivalent of a rocket-powered motorcycle and try to jump it. Many dollars have been spent on similar educational quick fixes, most turning into fads, and many ending with outcomes similar to Knievel's. Those failures are quantifiable, and the results are evident on a world stage. Our international rankings—especially in math and science—remain embarrassingly low.

Yet we are hardly stuck on one side of the educational canyon, looking longingly across to the other. A longer-lasting solution exists, and we don't have to move far from Evel Knievel's actual jump site to find a fitting metaphor. A little to the west lies the I. B. Perrine Bridge. It's a four-lane, truss-arch behemoth, rising 483 feet above the Snake and providing a vital link on trucker-dense U.S. Highway 93. The Perrine obviously took longer to construct than the Snake River Canyon jump took to fail, but it does its job solidly and has been in service in one form or another since 1927.

Spanning America's secondary education gap necessitates constructing a bridge using the steely girders of the formal cognitive neurosciences, not planning another jump. The goal is to create a system designed to support and improve executive function in teens in order to increase their academic performance. I've spent most of these pages trying to show why, from a brain science perspective, such an idea has a decent shot at bridging the distance.

My suggestions for aiding executive function sprinkled throughout this book are divisible into three learning environments: one for parents, one for teachers, one for teens.

Learning Environments for Parents

- Create a night school within an existing school for parents of students in a given district.
- Obtain certification for designated faculty who specialize in positive, evidence-based marital practice. Have them create a night school curriculum and then teach such practice to interested parents in the district.

Learning Environments for Teachers

- Work with a local college of education to create an evidence-based parenting curriculum to be inserted as a regular part of teacher training.
- When these teachers have graduated, enlist them as specialist faculty trained in evidence-based parenting practice.

Let them create a night school curriculum, and compensate them for this work and teaching such practices in the night school.
- Partner with these teachers and colleges to test the effectiveness of such coursework in different types of randomized, controlled experiments.

Learning Environments for Students

- Design a school whose centerpiece is a gym.
- Implement a physical movement curriculum based on protocols described in the text as a regular part of the school day. Encourage schoolwide participation in some kind of organized sport.
- Create a school start-time schedule that makes sense for adolescent brain development (8:30 start times for 10-year-olds, for example).
- Implement a nonoptional SEL program that passes the SAFE criteria mentioned in the text. Use one that specializes in empathy.
- Designate one room for regular mindfulness practice. Paint its walls green.
- Select a mindfulness-focused curriculum and certify instructors in its practice. Including the previously designed room, implement the practice schoolwide after testing for its effectiveness with adolescents.

Yes, we may need to take some of these ideas out for a long walk and have a heart-to-heart talk about practicality, for the proposed Better School for the Teen Brain comes with a few odd characteristics. One prominent feature is its involvement of a variety of players, from parents to teachers to entire colleges of education. It also requires lots of classwork for all, with courses ranging from evidence-based parenting practice to research-supported mindfulness meditation practices. A gym would be center stage, school start and end times would be radically different from the norm, and there'd be dedicated mindfulness-ready rooms fashioned into digital no-fly zones. Teachers would become educators of parents as well as students, and parents would become more active partners in the life of the school. It takes a lot of work to create an EF-friendly atmosphere, especially as students reach the age where their brains must endure their species-saving paroxysms of adolescence.

Would such a proposal be worth the cost of admission? It's certainly worth finding out. No middle or high school I know of was exclusively designed from the ground up to boost a teen's executive function, which means this book serves as one giant research proposal. Unfortunately, cognitive neuroscience labs and colleges of education don't regularly commingle, even though their interests often align (for instance, my office at the health sciences building at the University of Washington is almost a kilometer away from UW's College of Education). That's why the Better School for the Teen Brain is labeled as a "fantasy"—in the current educational climate, it has the real-world grounding of a Marvel comic book.

It doesn't have to be that way, of course. The aggregate findings of Planet Peer Review suggest that taking executive function seriously may be a fruitful endeavor. These issues really come home to me personally, not only because I've been interested in brain science and education for decades, but because this book was written while our two sons were both in their teens. As our family approaches the empty nest years, I have the luxurious terror of wondering about the educational world my grandkids—or anybody else's grandkids—will grow up in.

I think they'd do better on a bridge than they would on a two-wheeled rocket ship.

Acknowledgments

Thanks go to editors Susan Hills and Katie Martin—what fun this was to write!—and to the wonderful staff and support crew at ASCD. Gratitude also goes out to my two boys, both of whom were teens when this book was being written, and to my wife, for showing me these many years there is no statute of limitations on love. Or on patience.

Notes

Chapter 1

1. John Sowell, "Stuntman's Rocket Crosses Snake River Canyon, Where Knievel Had Failed," *Idaho Statesman*, September 15, 2016.

2. "2016 Tables: Institutions—Academic," *Nature Index*, accessed July 17, 2017, http://www.natureindex.com/annual-tables/2016/institution/all/all.

3. "Nobel Prize Winners by Country," *WorldAtlas*, accessed July 17, 2017, http://www.worldatlas.com/articles/top-30-countries-with-nobel-prize-winners.html.

4. "NAEP Long-Term Trend Assessments," *National Center for Education Statistics*, accessed July 17, 2017, http://nces.ed.gov/nationsreportcard/ltt/.

5. Ibid.

6. "PISA Tests: Top 40 for Maths and Reading," *BBC News*, October 14, 2015, http://www.bbc.com/news/business-26249042.

7. Laurence Steinberg, "What's Holding Back American Teenagers?" *Slate*, February 11, 2014, http://www.slate.com/articles/life/education/2014/02/high_school_in_america_a_complete_disaster.html.

8. Complete College America, *Remediation: Higher Education's Bridge to Nowhere* (Washington, DC: Author, 2012), http://www.completecollege.org/docs/CCA-Remediation-final.pdf.

9. Larry Gordon, "Remedial Courses Are 'Barriers' for Many Community College Students, Report Says," *EdSource*, November 9, 2016, https://edsource.org/2016/remedial-courses-are-barriers-for-many-community-college-students-report-says/572483/.

10. Jeffrey Selingo, "States Seek to Stiffen Their Admissions Standards," *Chronicle of Higher Education*, January 25, 2002.

11. Gordon, "Remedial Courses."

12. Alliance for Excellent Education, *Saving Now and Saving Later: How High School Reform Can Reduce the Nation's Wasted Remediation Dollars,* May 2011, https://all4ed.org/reports-factsheets/saving-now-and-saving-later-how-high-school-reform-can-reduce-the-nations-wasted-remediation-dollars/.

13. Sue Hendrickson, *Hunt for the Past: My Life as an Explorer* (New York: Cartwheel Books, 2001).

14. Walter Mischel, *The Marshmallow Test: Mastering Self-Control* (Boston: Little, Brown, 2014).

15. Walter Mischel, Yuichi Shoda, and Philip K. Peake, "The Nature of Adolescent Competencies Predicted by Preschool Delay of Gratification," *Journal of Personality and Social Psychology* 54, no. 4 (1988): 687–96.

16. Adele Diamond, "Executive Functions," *Annual Review of Psychology* 64 (2012): 135–68.

17. Alan Baddeley, "Working Memory: Theories, Models and Controversies," *Annual Review of Psychology* 63 (2012): 1–29.

18. "Executive Functioning: Skills Development Program," *Neuro Assessment & Development Center*, accessed January 5, 2018, http://www.neurodevelop.com/executive_functioning.

19. Baddeley, "Working Memory."

20. Alistair R. Evans, David Jones, Alison G. Boyer, James H. Brown, Daniel P. Costa, S. K. Morgan Ernest, Erich M. G. Fitzgerald, Mikael Fortelius, John L. Gittleman, Marcus J. Hamilton, Larisa E. Harding, Kari Lintulaakso, S. Kathleen Lyons, Jordan G. Okie, Juha J. Saarinen, Richard M. Sibly, Felisa A. Smith, Patrick R. Stephens, Jessica M. Theodor, and Mark D. Uhen, "The Maximum Rate of Mammal Evolution," *Proceedings of the National Academy of Sciences of the United States of America* 109, no. 11 (2012): 4187–90.

21. Naomi P. Friedman, Akira Miyake, Susan E. Young, John C. Defries, Robin P. Corley, and John K. Hewitt, "Individual Differences in Executive Functions Are Almost Entirely Genetic in Origin," *Journal of Experimental Psychology, General* 137, no. 2 (2008): 201–25.

22. Celeste Kidd, Holly Palmieri, and Richard N. Aslin, "Rational Snacking: Young Children's Decision-Making on the Marshmallow Task Is Moderated by Beliefs About Environmental Reliability," *Cognition* 126, no. 1 (2013): 109–14.

23. Andrew Lapin, "Teenage Eagle Hunter Is Mongolia's New Movie Star," *National Geographic*, August 4, 2016, http://news.nationalgeographic.com/2016/08/teenage-eagle-huntress-movie-trailer-director-interview/.

24. June P. Tangney, Roy F. Baumeister, and Angie Luzio Boone, "High Self-Control Predicts Good Adjustment, Less Pathology, Better Grades, and Interpersonal Success," *Journal of Personality* 72, no. 2 (2004): 271–324.

25. Roy F. Baumeister and John Tierney, *Willpower: Rediscovering the Greatest Human Strength* (New York: Penguin Press, 2011), 10.

26. Robin Jacob and Julia Parkinson, "The Potential for School-Based Interventions That Target Executive Function to Improve Academic Achievement: A Review," *Review of Educational Research* 85, no. 4 (2015): 512–52.

27. Rachelle H. Cantin, Emily K. Gnaedinger, Kristin C. Gallaway, Matthew S. Hesson-McInnis, and Alycia M. Hund, "Executive Functioning Predicts Reading, Mathematics, and Theory of Mind During the Elementary Years," *Journal of Experimental Child Psychology* 146 (2016): 66–78.

28. Audrey Breen, "Study Identifies a Key to Preventing Disruptive Behavior in Preschoolers," *Phys.org*, January 23, 2017, https://phys.org/news/2017-01-key-disruptive-behavior-preschool-classrooms.html.

29. Sheryl L. Olson, Arnold J. Sameroff, David C. R. Kerr, Nestor L. Lopez, and Henry M. Wellman, "Developmental Foundations of Externalizing Problems in Young Children: The Role of Effortful Control," *Development and Psychopathology* 17, no. 1 (2005): 25–45.

30. Lisa A. Jacobson, Amanda P. Williford, and Robert C. Pianta, "The Role of Executive Function in Children's Competent Adjustment to Middle School," *Child Neuropsychology* 17, no. 3 (2011): 255–80.

31. B. T. Conner et al. "Examining Self-Control as a Multidimensional Predictor of Crime and Drug Use in Adolescents with Criminal Histories," *Journal of Behavioral Health Service & Research* 36, no. 2 (2009): 137–49.

32. Amy Chua, *Battle Hymn of the Tiger Mother* (New York: Penguin Press, 2011).

33. "Battle Hymn of the Tiger Mother," *Wikipedia*, accessed July 27, 2017, https://en.wikipedia.org/wiki/Battle_Hymn_of_the_Tiger_Mother.

34. Tanith Carey, "Whatever Happened to the Original Tiger Mum's Children?" *The Telegraph* [U.K.], January 17, 2016, http://www.telegraph.co.uk/women/life/whatever-happened-to-the-original-tiger-mums-children/.

35. "PISA Tests," *BBC News*.

36. Laurence Steinberg, *Age of Opportunity: Lessons from the New Science of Adolescence* (Boston: Eamon Dolan/Houghton Mifflin Harcourt, 2014).

37. Carola Suárez-Orozco, Jean Rhodes, and Michael Millburn, "Unraveling the Immigrant Paradox," *Youth & Society* 41, no. 2 (2009): 151–85.

38. Tyler Vigen, "Spurious Correlations," accessed July 17, 2017, http://tylervigen.com/spurious-correlations.

39. T. E. Moffitt et al., "A Gradient of Childhood Self-Control Predicts Health, Wealth and Public Safety," *Proceedings of the National Academy of Sciences of the United States of America* 108, no.7 (2010): 2693–98.

Chapter 2

1. "Teen Dies 'Imitating *Jackass* Movie Stunt,'" *IOL*, December 18, 2002, http://www.iol.co.za/news/world/teen-dies-imitating-jackass-movie-stunt-98887.

2. BJ Casey and Kristina Caudle, "The Teenage Brain: Self Control," *Current Directions in Psychological Science* 22, no. 2 (2013): 82–87.

3. Scott Wise, "Teens Rescue 93-Year-Old Woman from Flooded Home," WTVR, November 2, 2015, http://wtvr.com/2015/11/02/teens-rescue-93-year-old-woman-from-flooded-home/.

4. University of Utah Neuroscience Initiative, "The Unfixed Brain," YouTube video, January 9, 2013, https://www.youtube.com/watch?v=jHxyP-nUhUY.

5. Eric H. Chudler, "Neurons," Brain Facts and Figures, accessed August 1, 2017, https://faculty.washington.edu/chudler/facts.html#neuron.

6. Eric H. Chudler, "Neuroanatomical, Neurophysiological and Neuropsychological Terminology," accessed August 1, 2017, https://faculty.washington.edu/chudler/neuroroot.html.

7. Andrew Koob and Jonah Lehrer, "The Root of Thought: What Do Glial Cells Do?" *Scientific American,* accessed August 1, 2017, https://www.scientificamerican.com/article/the-root-of-thought-what/.

8. Eric R. Kandel and A. J. Hudspeth, "The Brain and Behavior," in *Principles of Neural Science,* 5th ed., ed. Eric R. Kandel, James H. Schwartz, Thomas M. Jessell, Steven A. Siegelbaum, and A. J. Hudspeth, (New York: McGraw-Hill, 2013), 5–20.

9. Stephen G. Waxman, "Determinants of Conduction Velocity in Myelinated Nerve Fibers," *Muscle & Nerve* 3, no. 2 (1980): 141–50.

10. Lars T. Westlye, Kristine B. Walhovd, Anders M. Dale, Atle Bjørnerud, Paulina Due-Tønnessen, Andreas Engvig, Håkon Grydeland, Christian K. Tamnes, Ylva Østby, and Anders M. Fjell, "Life-Span Changes of the Human Brain White Matter: Diffusion Tensor Imaging (DTI) and Volumetry," *Cerebral Cortex* 20, no. 9 (2010): 2055–68.

11. Min Fu and Yi Zuo, "Experience-Dependent Structural Plasticity in the Cortex," *Trends in Neurosciences* 34, no. 4 (2011): 177–87.

12. Alex Fornito, Andrew Zalesky, and Michael Breakspear, "The Connectomics of Brain Disorders," *Nature Reviews. Neuroscience* 16, no. 3 (2015): 159–72; Miao Cao, Hao Huang, Yun Peng, Qi Dong, and Yong He, "Toward Developmental Connectomics of the Human Brain," *Frontiers in Neuroanatomy* 10 (2016). doi: 10.3389/fnana.2016.00025.

13. "*Gladiator* Mistake," YouTube video, posted by ashfan12, June 30, 2008, https://www.youtube.com/watch?v=vnij-xiPp_M.

14. Shazia Veqar Siddiqui, Ushri Chatterjee, Devvarta Kumar, Aleem Siddiqui, and Nishant Goyal, "Neuropsychology of Prefrontal Cortex," *Indian Journal of Psychiatry* 50, no. 3 (2008): 202–8.

15. P. Ratiu, et al., "The Tale of Phineas Gage, Digitally Remastered," *Journal of Neurotrauma* 21, no. 5 (2004): 637–43.

16. Helen Barbas, "General Cortical and Special Prefrontal Connections: Principles from Structure to Function," *Annual Review of Neuroscience* 38 (2015): 269–89.

17. Joseph E. LeDoux and Antonio R. Damasio, "Emotions and Feelings," in *Principles of Neural Science,* 5th ed., ed. Eric R. Kandel, James H. Schwartz, Thomas M. Jessell, Steven A. Siegelbaum, and A. J. Hudspeth (New York: McGraw-Hill, 2013), 5–20.

18. Daniel Strueber, Monika Lueck, and Gerhard Roth, "The Violent Brain," *Scientific American Mind* 17, no. 6 (2006): 20–27.

19. Nita Lelyveld, "Great Read: The Mad Scientists Behind the Zonk Prizes on 'Let's Make a Deal,'" *Los Angeles Times,* October 17, 2014, http://www.latimes.com/local/great-reads/la-me-c1-beat-lets-make-a-deal-zonks-20141017-story.html.

20. Clancy Blair, "Developmental Science and Executive Function," *Current Directions in Psychological Science* 25, no. 1 (2016): 3–7.

21. Anastasia Christakou, Mick Brammer, and Katya Rubia, "Maturation of Limbic Corticostriatal Activation and Connectivity Associated with Developmental Changes in Temporal Discounting," *NeuroImage* 54, no. 2 (2011): 1344–54.

22. Joseph Henrich, Steven J. Heine, and Ara Norenzayan, "The Weirdest People in the World?" *The Behavioral and Brain Sciences* 33, nos. 2–3 (2010): 61–135.

23. C. Cybele Raver, Clancy Blair, Michael Willoughby, and The Family Life Project Key Investigators, "Poverty as a Predictor of 4-Year-Olds' Executive Function: New Perspectives on Models of Differential Susceptibility," *Developmental Psychology* 49, no. 2 (2013): 292–304; Jamie L. Hanson, Moo K. Chung, Brian B. Avants, Elizabeth A. Shirtcliff, James C. Gee, Richard J. Davidson, and Seth D. Pollak, "Early Stress Is Associated with Alterations in the Orbitofrontal Cortex: A Tensor-Based Morphometry Investigation of Brain Structure and Behavioral Risk," *Journal of Neuroscience* 30, no. 22 (2010): 7466–72.

24. Heather P. Whitley and Wesley Lindsey, "Sex-Based Differences in Drug Activity," *American Family Physician* 80, no. 11 (2009): 1254–58.

25. Constance Holden, "Sex and the Suffering Brain," *Science* 308, no. 5728 (2005): 1574.

Chapter 3

1. Gonzalo Alvarez, Francisco C. Ceballos, and Celsa Quinteiro, "The Role of Inbreeding in the Extinction of a European Royal Dynasty," *PLOS One* 4, no. 4 (2009): e5174. doi: 10.1371/journal.pone.0005174.

2. Petra S. Hüppi, Simon Warfield, Ron Kikinis, Patrick D. Barnes, Gary P. Zientara, Farenc A. Jolesz, Miles K. Tsuji, and Joseph J. Volpe, "Quantitative Magnetic Resonance Imaging of Brain Development in Premature and Mature Newborns," *Annals of Neurology* 43, no. 2 (1998): 224–35; Peter R. Huttenlocher, "Morphometric Study of Human Cerebral Cortex Development," *Neuropsychologia* 28, no. 6 (1990): 517–27; John Easton, "Peter Huttenlocher, Pediatric Neurologist, 1931–2013," *UChicagoNews*, August 19, 2013, https://news.uchicago.edu/article/2013/08/19/peter-huttenlocher-pediatric-neurologist-1931-2013.

3. Sophie Messager, Emmanouella E. Chatzidaki, Dan Ma, Alan G. Hendrick, Dirk Zahn, John Dixon, Rosemary R. Thresher, Isabelle Malinge, Didier Lomet, Mark B. L. Carlton, William H. Colledge, Alain Caraty, and Samuel A. J. R. Aparicio, "Kisspeptin Directly Stimulates Gonadotropin-Releasing Hormone Release via G Protein-Coupled Receptor 54," *Proceedings of the National Academy of Sciences of the United States of America* 102, no. 5 (2005): 1761–66.

4. U.S. Department of Health and Human Services, Office on Women's Health, "Menstruation and the Menstrual Cycle Fact Sheet," *Womenshealth.gov*, October 21, 2009, https://www.womenshealth.gov/menstrual-cycle; Danielle E. Buttke, Kanta Sircar, and Colleen Martin, "Exposures to Endocrine-Disrupting Chemicals and Age of Menarche in Adolescent Girls in NHANES (2003–2008)," *Environmental Health Perspectives* 120, no. 11 (2012): 1613–18.

5. Sara B. Johnson, Robert W. Blum, and Jay N. Giedd, "Adolescent Maturity and the Brain: The Promise and Pitfalls of Neuroscience Research in Adolescent Health Policy," *Journal of Adolescent Health* 45, no. 3 (2009): 216–21; Emily L. Dennis, Neda Jahanshad, Katie L. McMahon, Greig I. de Zubicaray, Nicholas G. Martin, Ian B. Hickie, Arthur W. Toga, Margaret J. Wright, and Paul M. Thompson, "Development of Brain Structural Connectivity Between Ages 12 and 30: A 4-Tesla Diffusion Imaging Study in 439 Adolescents and Adults," *Neuroimage* 64 (2013): 671–84.

6. Dan Siegel, "The Power and Purpose of the Teenage Brain," accessed August 31, 2017, http://www.allreadable.com/7e10CHVl.

7. Jay N. Giedd, "The Teen Brain: Insights from Neuroimaging," *Journal of Adolescent Health* 42, no. 4 (2008): 335–43.

8. Ibid.

9. Olivia E. Coolidge, *Greek Myths*. (Boston: Houghton Mifflin, 1977).

10. Giedd, "The Teen Brain."

11. *"Emperor's New Groove* (1/8) Best Movie Quote—Kronk's Shoulder Angel and Devil (2000)," YouTube video, posted by Best Movie Quote, March 16, 2014, https://www.youtube.com/watch?v=RseLZ9LqQv0.

12. Kathryn L. Mills, Anne-Lise Goddings, Liv S. Clasen, Jay N. Giedd, and Sarah-Jayne Blakemore, "The Developmental Mismatch in Structural Brain Maturation During Adolescence," *Developmental Neuroscience* 36, nos. 3–4 (2014): 147–60.

13. Gary Olsen, "Parenting," accessed August 5, 2017, http://www.garyolsencartoons.com/parenting/index.htm.

14. Yang Qu, Adriana Galvan, Andrew J. Fuligni, Matthew D. Lieberman, and Eva H. Telzer, "Longitudinal Changes in Prefrontal Cortex Activation Underlie Declines in Adolescent Risk Taking," *Journal of Neuroscience* 35, no. 32 (2015): 11308–14.

15. Mills et al., "The Developmental Mismatch."

16. Rhoshel K. Lenroot and Jay N. Giedd, "Sex Differences in the Adolescent Brain," *Brain and Cognition* 72, no. 1 (2010): 46–55.

17. Elizabeth P. Shulman, K. Paige Harden, Jason M. Chein, and Laurence Steinberg, "Sex Differences in the Developmental Trajectories of Impulse Control and Sensation-Seeking from Early Adolescence to Early Adulthood," *Journal of Youth and Adolescence* 44, no. 1 (2015): 1–17.

18. University of Gothenberg, "No Gender Difference in Risk-Taking Behavior, Study Suggests," *Science Daily,* June 10, 2011, http://www.sciencedaily.com/releases/2011/06/110608081555.htm.

19. Jay N. Giedd, Matcheri Keshavan, and Tomáš Paus, "Why Do Many Psychiatric Disorders Emerge During Adolescence?" *Nature Review Neuroscience* 9, no. 12 (2008): 947–57.

20. Constance Holden, "Sex and the Suffering Brain," *Science* 308, no. 5728 (2005): 1574.

21. "A Christmas Story—The Triple Dog Dare Clip (HD)," YouTube video, posted by MrHDmovieclips, November 28, 2014, https://www.youtube.com/watch?v=qeJXYhdfR6Q.

22. Laurence Steinberg, "Cognitive and Affective Development in Adolescence," *Trends in Cognitive Sciences* 9, no. 2 (2005): 69–74.

23. Rebecca J. Johnson, Kevin D. McCaul, and William M. P. Klein, "Risk Involvement and Risk Perception Among Adolescents and Young Adults," *Journal of Behavioral Medicine* 25, no. 1 (2002): 67–82.

24. Valerie F. Reyna and Frank Farley, "Risk and Rationality in Adolescent Decision Making: Implications for Theory, Practice, and Public Policy," *Psychological Science in the Public Interest* 7, no. 1 (2006): 1–44.

25. Jason Chein, Dustin Albert, Lia O'Brien, Kaitlyn Uckert, and Laurence Steinberg, "Peers Increase Adolescent Risk Taking by Enhancing Activity in the Brain's Reward Circuitry," *Developmental Science* 14, no. 2 (2011): F1–F10; Laurence Steinberg and Kathryn C. Monahan, "Age Differences in Resistance to Peer Influence," *Developmental Psychology* 43, no. 6 (2007): 1531–43.

26. *"Footloose* (6/7) Movie Clip—Forgive Me Father (1984) HD," YouTube video, posted by Movieclips, October 10, 2011, https://www.youtube.com/watch?v=I6_C4fK94-c.

27. Gillian R. Brown and Peter J. Richerson, "Applying Evolutionary Theory to Human Behaviour: Past Differences and Current Debates," *Journal of Bioeconomics* 16, no. 2 (2014), 105–28. doi: 10.1007/s10818-013-9166-4.

28. Jay N. Giedd, "The Amazing Teen Brain," *Scientific American* 312, no. 6 (2015): 32–37.

Chapter 4

1. Isaac Asimov, *Futuredays: A Nineteenth-Century Vision of the Year 2000* (New York: Holt, 1986).

2. Simon Ramo, "A New Technique of Education," *Engineering and Science* 21 (1957): 17–22.

3. Matt Novak, "The Jetsons Get Schooled: Robot Teachers in the 21st Century Classroom," *Smithsonian.com,* March 29, 2013, http://www.smithsonianmag.com/history/the-jetsons-get-schooled-robot-teachers-in-the-21st-century-classroom-11797516/.

4. Ker Than, "Elephants Took 24 Million Generations to Evolve from Mouse-Size," *National Geographic*, February 4, 2012, http://news.nationalgeographic.com/news/2012/02/120203-mammals-evolution-body-size-science-elephants-mice/.

5. Robin I. M. Dunbar, "The Social Brain Hypothesis," *Evolutionary Anthropology* 6, no. 5 (1998): 178–90; Roger Lewin, *Human Evolution: An Illustrated Introduction*, 5th ed. (Malden, MA: Wiley-Blackwell, 2004).

6. Patrick Perry, "Norman Rockwell's Four Freedoms," *Saturday Evening Post*, January 1, 2009, http://www.saturdayeveningpost.com/2009/01/01/art-entertainment/norman-rockwell-art-entertainment/rockwells-four-freedoms.html.

7. Inge Bretherton, "The Origins of Attachment Theory: John Bowlby and Mary Ainsworth," *Developmental Psychology* 28, no. 5 (1992): 759–75.

8. Jeffery Liew, "Effortful Control, Executive Functions, and Education: Bringing Self-Regulatory and Social-Emotional Competencies to the Table," *Child Development Perspectives* 6, no. 2 (2012): 105–11.

9. Rory T. Devine, Giacomo Bignardi, and Claire Hughes, "Executive Function Mediates the Relations Between Parental Behaviors and Children's Early Academic Ability," *Frontiers in Psychology* 7 (2016): 1902.

10. Maximilian B. Bibok, Jeremy I. M. Carpendale, and Ulrich Müller, "Parental Scaffolding and the Development of Executive Function," *New Directions for Child and Adolescent Development* 2009, no. 123 (2009): 17–34.

11. Tracey Fay-Stammbach, David J. Hawes, and Pamela Meredith, "Parenting Influences on Executive Function in Early Childhood: A Review," *Child Development Perspectives* 8, no. 4 (2014): 258–64.

12. Margarita Azmitia, Catherine R. Cooper, and Jane R. Brown, "Support and Guidance from Families, Friends, and Teachers in Latino Early Adolescents' Math Pathways," *Journal of Early Adolescence* 29, no. 1 (2009): 142–69. doi: 10.1177/0272431608324476.

13. Laurence Steinberg, *Adolescence*, 11th ed. (New York: McGraw-Hill Education, 2016), 329.

14. David Mikkelson, "Fred Rogers—'Look for the Helpers,'" *Snopes.com*, May 23, 2017, http://www.snopes.com/look-for-the-helpers/.

15. Diana Baumrind, "Parental Disciplinary Patterns and Social Competence in Children," *Youth & Society* 9, no. 3 (1978): 239–67; Diana Baumrind, "Effects of Authoritative Parental Control on Child Behavior," *Child Development* 37, no. 4 (1966): 887–907.

16. Diana Baumrind, "The Influence of Parenting Style on Adolescent Competence and Substance Use," *Journal of Early Adolescence* 11, no. 1 (1991): 56–95.

17. Steinberg, *Adolescence,* 107.

18. Ali Alami, Shahla Khosravan, Leila Sadegh Moghadam, Fateme Pakravan, and Fateme Hosseni "Adolescents' Self-Esteem in Single and Two-Parent Families," *International Journal of Community Based Nursing and Midwifery* 2, no. 2 (2014): 69–76. doi: 10.2307/1131532.

19. Laurence Steinberg, Susie D. Lamborn, Sanford M. Dornbusch, and Nancy Darling, "Impact of Parenting Practices on Adolescent Achievement: Authoritative Parenting, School Involvement, and Encouragement to Succeed," *Child Development* 63, no. 5 (1992): 1266–81.

20. Cecilia Sin-Sze Cheung, Eva M. Pomerantz, and Wei Dong, "Does Adolescents' Disclosure to Their Parents Matter for Their Academic Adjustment?" *Child Development* 84, no. 2 (2013): 693–710; Nancy E. Hill and Ming-Te Wang, "From Middle School to College: Developing Aspirations, Promoting Engagement, and Indirect Pathways from Parenting to Post High School Enrollment," *Developmental Psychology* 51, no. 2 (2015): 224–35.

21. Lindsey Hutchison, Michael Feder, Beau Abar, and Adam Winsler, "Relations Between Parenting Stress, Parenting Style, and Child Executive Functioning for Children with ADHD or Autism," *Journal of Child and Family Studies* 25, no. 12 (2016): 3644–56.

22. Steinberg, *Adolescence,* 106.

23. Marc H. Bornstein, Chun-Shin Hahn, and Dieter Wolke, "Systems and Cascades in Cognitive Development and Academic Achievement," *Child Development* 84, no. 1 (2013): 154–62.

24. David J. Bridgett, Nicole M. Burt, Erin S. Edwards, and Kirby Deater-Deckard, "Intergenerational Transmission of Self-Regulation: A Multidisciplinary Review and Integrative Conceptual Framework," *Psychological Bulletin* 141, no. 3 (2015): 602–54; Mona El-Sheikh and Stephen A. Erath, "Family Conflict, Autonomic Nervous System Functioning, and Child Adaptation: State of the Science and Future Directions," *Development and Psychopathology* 23, no. 2 (2011): 703–21.

25. Kathleen McCoy, E. Mark Cummings, and Patrick T. Davies, "Constructive and Destructive Marital Conflict, Emotional Security and Children's Prosocial Behavior," *Journal of Child Psychology and Psychiatry* 50, no. 3 (2009): 270–79.

26. John Mordechai Gottman and Robert Wayne Levenson, "A Two-Factor Model for Predicting When a Couple Will Divorce: Exploratory Analyses Using 14-Year Longitudinal Data," *Family Process* 41, no. 1 (2002): 83–96.

27. John M. Gottman and Nan Silver, *The Seven Principles for Making Marriage Work* (New York: Three Rivers Press, 2000).

28. John M. Gottman and Robert W. Levenson, "Marital Processes Predictive of Later Dissolution: Behavior, Physiology, and Health," *Journal of Personality and Social Psychology* 63, no. 2 (1992): 221–33.

29. Thomas H. Maugh II, "Men, Here Are the Magic Words to Long Marriages: Yes, Dear," *Seattle Times*, February 21, 1998, http://community.seattletimes.nwsource.com/archive/?date=19980221&slug=2735662.

30. Beverly J. Wilson and John M. Gottman, "Marital Conflict, Repair, and Parenting," in *Handbook of Parenting, Vol. 4. Social Conditions and Applied Parenting*, 2nd ed., ed. Marc H. Bornstein (Mahwah, NJ: Erlbaum, 2002), 227–58.

Chapter 5

1. Elizabeth Street, "The Moving Story of How a Teacher Inspired Maya Angelou to Speak," *Learning Liftoff*, May 8, 2017, http://www.learningliftoff.com/how-a-teacher-inspired-maya-angelou-to-speak/WhrUj7Q-eu4; *Fresh Air*, "'Fresh Air' Remembers Poet and Memoirist Maya Angelou," NPR, May 28, 2014, http://www.npr.org/2014/05/28/316707321/fresh-air-remembers-poet-and-memoirist-maya-angelou.

2. Jacquelynne S. Eccles and Robert W. Roeser, "Schools as Developmental Contexts During Adolescence," *Journal of Research on Adolescence* 21, no. 1 (2011): 225–41.

3. Laurence Steinberg, *Adolescence,* 11th ed. (New York: McGraw-Hill Education, 2016), 169–70; Jacquelynne S. Eccles, "Schools, Academic Motivation, and Stage-Environment Fit," in *Handbook of Adolescent Psychology,* ed. Richard M. Lerner and Laurence Steinberg (Hoboken, NJ: John Wiley & Sons, 2004), 125–53.

4. Christopher P. Niemiec and Richard M. Ryan, "Autonomy, Competence, and Relatedness in the Classroom: Applying Self-Determination Theory to Educational Practice," *Theory and Research in Education* 7, no. 2 (2009), 133–44.

5. *English Oxford Living Dictionaries,* s.v. "expectation," accessed October 15, 2017, https://en.oxforddictionaries.com/definition/expectation.

6. "Valentines Day Card from a Student," *Reddit* post, posted by hate_mail, February 15, 2017, https://www.reddit.com/r/funny/comments/5u81i3/valentines_day_card_from_a_student/.

7. Robert Rosenthal and Lenore Jacobson, *Pygmalion in the Classroom: Teacher Expectation and Pupils' Intellectual Development* (Bethel, CT: Crown House, 2003).

8. Alix Spiegel, "Teachers' Expectations Can Influence How Students Perform," NPR, September 17, 2012, http://www.npr.org/sections/health-shots/2012/09/18/161159263/teachers-expectations-can-influence-how-students-perform.

9. Nicole S. Sorhagen, "Early Teacher Expectations Disproportionately Affect Poor Children's High School Performance," *Journal of Educational Psychology* 105, no. 2 (2013): 465–77.

10. Dominik Becker, "The Impact of Teachers' Expectations on Students' Educational Opportunities in the Life Course: An Empirical Test of a Subjective Expected Utility Explanation," *Rationality and Society* 25, no. 4 (2013): 422–69.

11. Steinberg, *Adolescence,* 170.

12. Jorie Koster-Hale and Rebecca Saxe, "Theory of Mind: A Neural Prediction Problem," *Neuron* 79, no. 5 (2013): 836–48.

13. Simon Baron-Cohen, Sally Wheelwright, Jacqueline Hill, Yogini Raste, and Ian Plumb. "The 'Reading the Mind in the Eyes' Test Revised Version: A Study with Normal Adults, and Adults with Asperger Syndrome or High-Functioning Autism." *Journal of Child Psychology and Psychiatry* 42 (2001): 241–51.

14. David Comer Kidd and Emanuele Castano, "Reading Literary Fiction Improves Theory of Mind," *Science* 342, no. 6156 (2013): 377–80.

15. Jamie Robert Vollmer, "The Blueberry Story," *Education Week,* March 6, 2002.

16. Maureen T. Hallinan, "Teacher Influences on Students' Attachment to School," *Sociology of Education* 81, no. 3 (2008): 271–83.

17. Claudia M. Mueller and Carol S. Dweck, "Praise for Intelligence Can Undermine Children's Motivation and Performance," *Journal of Personality and Social Psychology* 75, no. 1 (1998), 33–52.

18. Eccles, "Schools, Academic Motivation, and Stage-Environment Fit."

19. Joseph P. Allen, Robert C. Pianta, Anne Gregory, Amori Yee Mikami, and Janetta Lun, "An Interaction-Based Approach to Enhancing Secondary School Instruction and Student Achievement," *Science* 333, no. 6045 (2011): 1034–37.

20. Douglas A. Bernstein, "Parenting and Teaching: What's the Connection in Our Classrooms?" *American Psychological Association*, September 2013, http://www.apa.org/ed/precollege/ptn/2013/09/parenting-teaching.aspx.

21. Samantha W. Bindman, Eva M. Pomerantz, and Glenn I. Roisman, "Do Children's Executive Functions Account for Associations Between Early Autonomy-Supportive Parenting and Achievement Through High School?" *Journal of Educational Psychology* 107, no. 3 (2015): 756–70.

22. Steinberg, *Adolescence*, 171.

23. Natasha Hinde, "Teacher Moved to Tears by Heartfelt Letter from Pupil Who Thanked Him for Being 'Like a Dad' to Him," *Huffington Post UK*, April 25, 2017, http://www.huffingtonpost.co.uk/entry/teacher-moved-to-tears-by-letter-from-pupil-likening-him-to-the-dad-he-never-met_uk_58ff0765e4b0288f5dc7a139.

24. Robin Marantz Henig "Understanding the Anxious Mind," *New York Times Magazine*, September 29, 2009, http://www.nytimes.com/2009/10/04/magazine/04anxiety-t.html; Jerome Kagan and Nancy Snidman, *The Long Shadow of Temperament,* (Cambridge, MA: Belknap Press, 2009), 56, 217–30.

25. Bernstein, "Parenting and Teaching."

Chapter 6

1. Eric Schwartz, "For Jason Garstkiewicz, Surviving Cancer Was Just the First Step," *Haddonfield Patch*, October 4, 2012, https://patch.com/new-jersey/haddon/for-jason-garstkiewicz-surviving-cancer-was-just-the-first-step.

2. U.S. Department of Health and Human Services, Centers for Disease Control and Prevention, National Center for Chronic Disease Prevention and Health Promotion, and The President's Council on Physical Fitness and Sports, "Physical Activity and Health: Adolescents and Young Adults," accessed August 8, 2017, https://www.cdc.gov/nccdphp/sgr/pdf/adoles.pdf.

3. Palo Alto Medical Foundation, "Teen Obesity," accessed August 8, 2017, http://www.pamf.org/teen/health/diseases/obesity.html.

4. Joe Donatelli, "The 19 Funniest Fitness Fads of All Time," *Livestrong.com,* March 16, 2017, http://www.livestrong.com/slideshow/1011141-19-funniest-fitness-fads-time-now.

5. Danielle Laurin, René Verreault, Joan Lindsay, Kathleen MacPherson, and Kenneth Rockwood, "Physical Activity and Risk of Cognitive Impairment and Dementia in Elderly Persons," *Archives of Neurology* 58, no. 3 (2001): 498–504.

6. Stanley Colcombe and Arthur F. Kramer, "Fitness Effects on the Cognitive Function of Older Adults: A Meta-Analytic Study," *Psychological Science* 14, no. 2 (2003): 125–30; Cédric T. Albinet, Geoffroy Boucard, Cédric A. Bouquet, and Michel Audiffren,

"Increased Heart Rate Variability and Executive Performance After Aerobic Training in the Elderly," *European Journal of Applied Physiology* 109, no. 4 (2010): 617–24.

7. Adam G. Thomas, Andrea Dennis, Peter A. Bandettini, and Heidi Johansen-Berg, "The Effects of Aerobic Activity on Brain Structure," *Frontiers in Psychology* 3 (2012): 86. doi: 10.3389/fpsyg.2012.00086.

8. Michelle W. Voss, Ruchika S. Prakash, Kirk I. Erickson, Chandramallika Basak, Laura Chaddock, Jennifer S. Kim, Heloisa Alves, Susie Heo, Amanda N. Szabo, Siobhan M. White, Thomas R. Wójcicki, Emily L. Mailey, Neha Gothe, Erin A. Olson, Edward McAuley, and Arthur F. Kramer, "Plasticity of Brain Networks in a Randomized Intervention Trial of Exercise Training in Older Adults," *Frontiers in Aging Neuroscience* 2 (2010): 32. doi: 10.3389/fnagi.2010.00032.

9. Kirk I. Erickson, Michelle W. Voss, Ruchika Shaurya Prakesh, Chandramallika Basak, Amanda Szabo, Laura Chaddock, Jennifer S. Kim, Susie Heo, Heloisa Alves, Siobhan M. White, Thomas R. Wójcicki, Emily Mailey, Victoria J. Vieira, Stephen A. Martin, Brandt D. Pence, Jeffrey A. Woods, Edward McAuley, and Arthur F. Kramer, "Exercise Training Increases Size of Hippocampus and Improves Memory," *Proceedings of the National Academy of Sciences of the United States of America* 108, no. 7 (2011): 3017–22.

10. Claudia Voelcker-Rehage and Claudia Niemann, "Structural and Functional Brain Changes Related to Different Types of Physical Activity Across the Life Span," *Neuroscience and Biobehavioral Reviews* 37, no. 9, part B (2013): 2268–95.

11. Suvi Rovio, Ingemar Kåreholt, Eeva-Liisa Helkala, Matti Viitanen, Bengt Winblad, Jaakko Tuomilehto, Hilkka Soininen, Aulikki Nissinen, and Miia Kivipelto, "Leisure-Time Physical Activity at Midlife and the Risk of Dementia and Alzheimer's Disease," *The Lancet Neurology* 4, no. 11 (2005): 705–7.

12. Charles Hillman and S. M. Buck, "Physical Fitness and Cognitive Function in Healthy Pre-Adolescent Children" (paper presented at the Annual Meeting of the Society for Psychophysiological Research, Santa Fe, NM, October 2004).

13. Hayley Guiney and Liana Machado, "The Benefits of Regular Aerobic Exercise for Executive Functioning in Healthy Populations," *Psychonomic Bulletin & Review* 20, no. 1 (2013): 73–66.

14. BBC News Scotland, "Exercise 'Boosts Academic Performance' of Teenagers," October 23, 2013, http://www.bbc.com/news/uk-scotland-24608813.

15. Michele Tine, "Acute Aerobic Exercise: An Intervention for the Selective Visual Attention and Reading Comprehension of Low-Income Adolescents," *Frontiers in Psychology* 5 (2014): 575. doi: 10.3389/fpsyg.2017.00632.

16. Caitlin Lees and Jessica Hopkins, "Effect of Aerobic Exercise on Cognition, Academic Achievement, and Psychosocial Function in Children: A Systematic Review of Randomized Control Trials," *Preventing Chronic Disease* 10 (2013). doi: 10.5888/pcd10.130010.

17. Celia Álvarez-Bueno, Caterina Pesce, Iván Cavero-Redondo, Mairena Sánchez-López, María Jesús Pardo-Guijarro, and Vicente Martínez-Vizcaíno, "Association of Physical Activity with Cognition, Metacognition and Academic Performance in Children and Adolescents: A Protocol for Systematic Review and Meta-Analysis," *BMJ Open* 6, no. 6 (2016): e011065. doi: 10.1136/bmjopen-2016-011065.

18. Megan M. Herting and Bonnie J. Nagel, "Differences in Brain Activity During a Verbal Associative Memory Encoding Task in High- and Low-Fit Adolescents," *Journal of Cognitive Neuroscience* 25, no. 4 (2013): 595–612.

19. Adele Diamond and Daphne S. Ling, "Conclusions About Interventions, Programs, and Approaches for Improving Executive Functions That Appear Justified and Those That, Despite Much Hype, Do Not," *Developmental Cognitive Neuroscience* 18 (2016): 34–48.

20. John R. Best, "Effects of Physical Activity on Children's Executive Function: Contributions of Experimental Research on Aerobic Exercise," *Developmental Review* 30, no. 4 (2010): 331–51.

21. Caterina Pesce, Claudia Crova, Lucio Cereatti, Rita Casella, and Mario Bellucci, "Physical Activity and Mental Performance in Preadolescents: Effects of Acute Exercise on Free-Recall Memory," *Mental Health and Physical Activity* 2, no. 1 (2009): 16–22.

22. Diamond and Ling, "Conclusions."

23. Carmen Vivar, Michelle C. Potter, and Henriette van Praag, "All About Running: Synaptic Plasticity, Growth Factors and Adult Hippocampal Neurogenesis," *Current Topics in Behavioral Neurosciences* 15 (2013): 189–210.

24. Tim Bliss, Graham Collingridge, and Richard Morris, "Synaptic Plasticity in Health and Disease: Introduction and Overview," *Philosophical Transactions of the Royal Society of London. Series B, Biological Sciences* 369, no. 1633 (2014). doi: 10.1098/rstb.2013.0129.

25. Erickson et al., "Exercise Training."

26. Grace Sophia Griesbach, David Allen Hovda, and Fernando Gomez-Pinilla, "Exercise-Induced Improvement in Cognitive Performance After Traumatic Brain Injury in Rats Is Dependent on BDNF Activation," *Brain Research* 1288 (2009): 105–15.

27. Ana C. Pereira, Dan E. Huddleston, Adam M. Brickman, Alexander A. Sosunov, Rene Hen, Guy M. McKhann, Richard Sloan, Fred H. Gage, Truman R. Brown, and Scott A. Small, "An *In Vivo* Correlate of Exercise-Induced Neurogenesis in the Adult Dentate Gyrus," *Proceedings of the National Academy of Sciences of the United States of America* 104, no. 13 (2007), 5638–43.

28. Sheepsumon Viboolvorakul and Suthiluk Patumraj, "Exercise Training Could Improve Age-Related Changes in Cerebral Blood Flow and Capillary Vascularity Through the Upregulation of VEGF and ENOS," *BioMed Research International* 2014 (2014), ID 230791; Kechun Tang, Feng Cheng Xia, Peter D. Wagner, and Ellen C. Breen, "Exercise-Induced VEGF Transcriptional Activation in Brain, Lung and Skeletal Muscle," *Respiratory Physiology and Neurobiology* 170, no. 1 (2010): 16–22.

29. "Teens Write About Depression: D.'s Story," PBS, *In the Mix,* accessed August 8, 2017, http://www.pbs.org/inthemix/shows/show_depression5.html#dstory.

30. Centers for Disease Control, "Suicide: Facts at a Glance 2015," accessed August 8, 2017, https://www.cdc.gov/violenceprevention/pdf/suicide-datasheet-a.pdf.

31. National Institute of Mental Health, "Major Depression Among Adolescents," accessed August 8, 2017, https://www.nimh.nih.gov/health/statistics/prevalence/major-depression-among-adolescents.shtml.

32. Kirsten Weir, "The Exercise Effect," *American Psychological Association Monitor on Psychology* 42, no. 11 (2011): 48, http://www.apa.org/monitor/2011/12/exercise.aspx.

33. Tim Carter, Ioannis D. Morres, Oonagh Meade, and Patrick Callaghan, "The Effect of Exercise on Depressive Symptoms in Adolescents: A Systematic Review and Meta-Analysis," *Journal of the American Academy of Child and Adolescent Psychiatry* 55, no. 7 (2016): 580–90.

34. Leo Sher, "The Role of Brain-Derived Neurotrophic Factor in the Pathophysiology of Adolescent Suicidal Behavior," *International Journal of Adolescent Medicine and Health* 23, no. 3 (2011): 181–85.

35. M. Verhagen, A. van der Meij, P. A. M. van Deurzen, J. G. E. Janzing, A. Arias-Vásquez, J. K. Buitelaar, and B. Franke, "Meta-Analysis of the BDNF Val66Met Polymorphism in Major Depressive Disorder: Effects of Gender and Ethnicity," *Molecular Psychiatry* 15 (2010): 260–71.

36. R. N. Carmody and R.W. Wrangham. "Cooking and the Human Commitment to a High-Quality Diet." *Cold Spring Harbor Symposia on Quantitative Biology* 74 (2009): 427–34.

37. Jeri Brittin, Dina Sorensen, Karen K. Lee, Dieter Breithecker, Leah Frerichs, and Terry Huang, "Physical Activity Design Guidelines for School Architecture," *PLOS One,* (2015). doi.org/10.1371/journal.pone.0132597.

38. Centers for Disease Control and Prevention, "Physical Education Curriculum Analysis Tool (PECAT)," August 6, 2015, https://www.cdc.gov/healthyschools/pecat/index.htm.

Chapter 7

1. Esther Lee, "Matt Damon Talks About Daughters in Cute Interview, Eldest 'Just Got Her License,'" *Us Magazine,* September 25, 2015, http://www.usmagazine.com/celebrity-moms/news/matt-damon-talks-about-daughters-in-cute-new-interview-2015259.

2. Lisa Respers France, "Ben Affleck and Jennifer Garner's Friendly Divorce," *CNN Entertainment,* April 14, 2017, http://www.cnn.com/2017/04/14/entertainment/ben-affleck-jennifer-garner-divorce/index.html.

3. Bella DePaulo, "What Is the Divorce Rate, Really?" *Psychology Today,* February 2, 2017, https://www.psychologytoday.com/blog/living-single/201702/what-is-the-divorce-rate-really.

4. Hyun Sik Kim, "Consequences of Parental Divorce for Child Development," *American Sociological Review* 76, no. 3 (2011): 487–511.

5. Jennifer Weaver and Thomas Schofield, "Mediation and Moderation of Divorce Effects on Children's Behavior Problems," *Journal of Family Psychology: JFP: Journal of the Division of Family Psychology of the American Psychological Association (Division 43)* 29, no. 1 (2015): 39–48; "Effects of Divorce on Children's Social Skills," *Marripedia,* accessed August 8, 2017, http://www.marripedia.org/effects.of.divorce.on.children.s.social.skills.

6. David H. Demo and Alan C. Acock, "The Impact of Divorce on Children," *Journal of Marriage and the Family* 50, no. 3 (1988): 619–48.

7. Lisa Strohschein, "Parental Divorce and Child Mental Health Trajectories," *Journal of Marriage and the Family* 67, no. 5 (2005): 1286–300; Haley Robertson, "Exploring Potential Connections Between Parental Divorce, Deviance and Negative Child Outcomes: A Literature Review," accessed August 8, 2017, http://search.proquest.com/docview/1803233721; Hira Nair and Ann D. Murray, "Predictors of Attachment Security in Preschool Children from Intact and Divorced Families," *Journal of Genetic Psychology: Research and Theory on Human Development* 166, no. 3 (2005): 245–63.

8. Daniel L. Schacter, Daniel T. Gilbert, and Daniel M. Wegner, *Introducing Psychology* (New York: Worth, 2013), 319.

9. Joseph A. Durlak, Roger P. Weissberg, Allison B. Dymnicki, Rebecca D. Taylor, and Kriston B. Schellinger, "The Impact of Enhancing Students' Social and Emotional Learning: A Meta-Analysis of School-Based Universal Interventions," *Child Development* 82, no. 1 (2011): 405–32.

10. Laurence Steinberg, *Age of Opportunity: Lessons from the New Science of Adolescence* (New York: Houghton Mifflin Harcourt, 2015), 161.

11. Durlak et al., "The Impact of Enhancing."

12. Lynda A. Haynes and Arthur W. Avery, "Training Adolescents in Self-Disclosure and Empathy Skills," *Journal of Counseling Psychology* 26, no. 6 (1979): 526–30.

13. Martin L. Hoffman, *Empathy and Moral Development: Implications for Caring and Justice* (New York: Cambridge University Press, 2000).

14. Helen G. M. Vossen and Patti M. Valkenburg, "Do Social Media Foster or Curtail Adolescents' Empathy? A Longitudinal Study," *Computers in Human Behavior* 63 (2016): 118–24.

15. Delores Gallo, "Educating for Empathy, Reason and Imagination," *Journal of Creative Behavior* 23, no. 2 (1989): 98–115.

16. Jolien Van der Graaff, Susan Branje, Minet De Wied, Skyler Hawk, Pol Van Lier, and Wim Meeus, "Perspective Taking and Empathic Concern in Adolescence: Gender Differences in Developmental Changes," *Developmental Psychology* 50, no. 3 (2014): 881–88.

17. Lane Beckes, James A. Coan, and Karen Hasselmo, "Familiarity Promotes the Blurring of Self and Other in the Neural Representation of Threat," *Social Cognitive and Affective Neuroscience* 8, no. 6 (2013): 670–77.

18. "Dear Scout," Facebook post, posted by UNSW Love Letters, October 28, 2013, https://www.facebook.com/permalink.php?id=148144265354304&story_fbid=227835684051828.

19. Van der Graaff et al., "Perspective Taking."

20. Jean Decety, "The Neurodevelopment of Empathy in Humans," *Developmental Neuroscience* 32, no. 4 (2010): 257–67.

21. Eveline A. Crone and Ronald E. Dahl, "Understanding Adolescence as a Period of Social-Affective Engagement and Goal Flexibility," *Nature Reviews Neuroscience* 13, no. 9 (2012): 636–50.

22. Pew Research Center, "Social Media Fact Sheet," *Pew Research Center: Internet and Technology,* January 12, 2017, http://www.pewinternet.org/fact-sheet/social-media/.

23. Jeffrey Gottfried and Elisa Shearer, "News Use Across Social Media Platforms 2016," *Pew Research Center: Journalism and Media,* May 26, 2016, http://www.journalism.org/2016/05/26/news-use-across-social-media-platforms-2016/.

24. "Reach of Leading Social Media and Networking Sites Used by Teenagers and Young Adults in the United States as of February 2017," *Statista,* accessed August 8, 2017, https://www.statista.com/statistics/199242/social-media-and-networking-sites-used-by-us-teenagers/.

25. Hayley Tsukayama, "Teens Spend Nearly Nine Hours Every Day Consuming Media," *Washington Post*, November 3, 2015, https://www.washingtonpost.com/news/the-switch/wp/2015/11/03/teens-spend-nearly-nine-hours-every-day-consuming-media/.

26. Kara Fox, "Instagram Worst Social Media App for Young People's Mental Health," *CNN Health*, May 19, 2017, http://www.cnn.com/2017/05/19/health/instagram-worst-social-network-app-young-people-mental-health/index.html.

27. Vossen and Valkenburg, "Do Social Media."

28. Yalda T. Uhls, Minas Michikyan, Jordan Morris, Debra Garcia, Gary W. Small, Eleni Zgourou, and Patricia M. Greenfield, "Five Days at Outdoor Education Camp Without Screens Improves Preteen Skills with Nonverbal Emotion Cues," *Computers in Human Behavior* 39 (2014): 387–92.

29. "11 Alarm Clocks for Heavy Sleepers," *Health.com*, accessed August 8, 2017, http://www.health.com/health/gallery/0,,20506099,00.html; "21 Alarm Clocks You'd Definitely Want to Wake Up To," *BuzzFeed*, June 28, 2013, https://www.buzzfeed.com/ciarapavia/21-alarm-clocks-youd-definitely-want-to-wake-up-to?utm_term=.moPMjmBMD#.bnmKbvZKB; Charlie White, "Money-Shredding Alarm Clock Is Completely Unforgiving," *Mashable*, May 29, 2011, http://mashable.com/2011/05/29/money-shredding-alarm/.

30. American Academy of Pediatrics Adolescent Sleep Working Group, Committee on Adolescence, and Council on School Health, "Policy Statement: School Start Times for Adolescents," *Pediatrics* 134, no. 3 (2014): 642–49.

31. Paul Kelley, Steven W. Lockley, Russell G. Foster, and Jonathan Kelley, "Synchronizing Education to Adolescent Biology: 'Let Teens Sleep, Start School Later,'" *Learning, Media and Technology* 40, no. 2 (2015): 210–26.

32. "5 Pros and Cons of Later School Start Times," *Master of Arts in Teaching Guide*, accessed August 8, 2017, http://www.masterofartsinteaching.net/lists/5-pros-and-cons-of-later-school-start-times/.

33. Kyla L. Wahlstrom, Beverly J. Dretzke, Molly F. Gordon, Kristin Peterson, Katherine Edwards, and Julie Gdula, *Examining the Impact of Later School Start Times on the Health and Academic Performance of High School Students: A Multi-Site Study*, Center for Applied Research and Educational Improvement (St. Paul, MN: University of Minnesota, 2014).

34. Marco Hafner et al., "Later School Start Times in the U.S.," *Rand Corporation*, 2017, https://www.rand.org/pubs/research_reports/RR2109.html

Chapter 8

1. "*Fantastic Mr. Fox*," *IMDB*, accessed August 8, 2017, http://www.imdb.com/title/tt0432283/.

2. Sophie Bethune, "Teen Stress Rivals That of Adults," *American Psychological Association Monitor on Psychology* 45, no. 4 (2014): 20, http://www.apa.org/monitor/2014/04/teen-stress.aspx.

3. Susanna Schrobsdorff, "Teen Depression and Anxiety: Why the Kids Are Not Alright," *Time* 188, no. 19 (2016), http://time.com/4547322/american-teens-anxious-depressed-overwhelmed/; Kathleen Ries Merikangas et al., "Lifetime Prevalence of Mental Disorders in U.S. Adolescents, Results from the National Comorbidity Study—Adolescent Supplement (NCS-A)," *Journal of the Amercian Academy of Adolescent Psychiatry 49*, no. 10 (2010): 980–89.

4. Kathleen Ries Merikangas et al., "Service Utilization for Lifetime Mental Disorders in U.S. Adolescents Results from the National Comorbidity Study-Adolescent Supplement (NCS-A)," *Journal of the Amercian Academy of Adolescent Psychiatry* 50, no. 1, 32–45.

5. Schrobsdorff, "Teen Depression and Anxiety."

6. Sherrie Peif, "Family of Fatal Crash Victim: 'Never, Never Text and Drive,'" *The [Greeley, CO] Tribune*, April 19, 2013.

7. James W. Bisley, "The Neural Basis of Visual Attention," *Journal of Physiology* 589, pt. 1 (2011): 49–57; Narayanan Srinivasan, Priyanka Srivastava, Monika Lohani, and Shruti Baijal, "Focused and Distributed Attention," *Progress in Brain Research* 176 (2009): 87–100.

8. Daphne Bavelier and C. Shawn Green, "The Brain-Boosting Power of Video Games," *Scientific American* 315 (2016): 26–31.

9. Aaron Drummond and James D. Sauer, "Video-Games Do Not Negatively Impact Adolescent Academic Performance in Science, Mathematics or Reading," *PLOS One* 9, no. 4 (2014): e87943.

10. Kira Bailey, Robert West, Craig A. Anderson, "A Negative Association Between Video Game Experience and Proactive Cognitive Control," *Psychophysiology* 47, no. 1 (2010): 34–42.

11. Victoria L. Dunckley, "Gray Matters: Too Much Screen Time Damages the Brain," *Psychology Today*, February 27, 2014, https://www.psychologytoday.com/blog/mental-wealth/201402/gray-matters-too-much-screen-time-damages-the-brain.

12. Eyal Ophir, Clifford Nass, and Anthony D. Wagner, "Cognitive Control in Media Multitaskers," *Proceedings of the National Academy of Sciences of the United States of America* 106, no. 37 (2009): 15583–87.

13. Adam Gorlick, "Media Multitaskers Pay Mental Price, Stanford Study Shows," *Stanford News*, August 24, 2009, http://news.stanford.edu/2009/08/24/multitask-research-study-082409/.

14. Yi-Yuan Tang, Britta K. Hölzel, and Michael I. Posner, "The Neuroscience of Mindfulness Meditation," *Nature Reviews Neuroscience* 16 (2015): 213–25.

15. John Teasdale, Mark Williams, and Zindel Segal, *The Mindful Way Workbook* (New York: Guilford Press, 2014).

16. Stefan G. Hofmann, Alice T. Sawyer, Ashley A. Witt, and Diana Oh, "The Effect of Mindfulness-Based Therapy on Anxiety and Depression: A Meta-Analytic Review," *Journal of Consulting and Clinical Psychology* 78, no. 2 (2010): 169–83.

17. Tom Ireland, "What Does Mindfulness Meditation Do to Your Brain?" *Scientific American*, June 12, 2014, https://blogs.scientificamerican.com/guest-blog/what-does-mindfulness-meditation-do-to-your-brain/.

18. Eva Oberle, Kimberly A. Schonert-Reichl, Molly Stewart Lawlor, and Kimberly C. Thomson, "Mindfulness and Inhibitory Control in Early Adolescence," *Journal of Early Adolescence* 32, no. 4 (2012): 565–88.

19. Yi-Yuan Tang, Lizhu Yang, Leslie D. Leve, and Gordon T. Harold, "Improving Executive Function and Its Neurobiological Mechanisms Through a Mindfulness-Based Intervention: Advances Within the Field of Developmental Neuroscience," *Child Development Perspectives* 6, no. 4 (2012): 361–66.

20. J. David Creswell, "Mindfulness Interventions," *Annual Review of Psychology* 68 (2017): 491–516; Ireland, "Mindfulness."

21. Shahriar Sheikhbahaei and Jeffrey C. Smith, "Breathing to Inspire and Arouse," *Science* 355, no. 6332 (2017): 1370–71.

22. Kevanne Louise Sanger and Dusana Dorjee, "Mindfulness Training for Adolescents: A Neurodevelopmental Perspective on Investigating Modifications in Attention and Emotion Regulation Using Event-Related Brain Potentials," *Cognitive, Affective, & Behavioral Neuroscience* 15, no. 3 (2015): 696–711.

23. John H. Meiklejohn, Catherine Phillips, M. Lee Freedman, Mary Lee Griffin, Gina M. Biegel, Andrew T. Roach, Jennifer L. Frank, Christine Burke, Laura Pinger, Geoff Soloway, Roberta Isberg, Erica M. S. Sibinga, Laurie Grossman, and Amy Saltzman, "Integrating Mindfulness Training into K–12 Education: Fostering the Resilience of Teachers and Students," *Mindfulness* 3, no. 4 (2012): 291–307.

24. An extensive list of site-specific and online courses can be found at http://www.bu.edu/fsao/resources-for-mindfulness/. Information about a well-regarded program at the University of California, San Diego, resides at https://health.ucsd.edu/specialties/mindfulness/Pages/default.aspx. And information about another well-regarded program from University of Massachusetts Medical School is located at http://www.umassmed.edu/cfm.

25. Nancy M. Wells, "At Home with Nature: Effects of 'Greenness' on Children's Cognitive Function," *Environment and Behavior* 32, no. 6 (2000): 775–95; Andrea Faber Taylor, Frances E. Kuo, and William C. Sullivan, "Coping with ADD: The Surprising Connection to Green Play Settings," *Environment and Behavior* 33, no. 1 (2001): 54–77.

Index

Note: Page references followed by an italicized *f* indicate information contained in figures.

About the Author

 **Dr. John J. Medina** is a developmental molecular biologist with special research interests in the isolation and characterization of genes involved in human brain development and the genetics of psychiatric disorders. Medina has spent most of his professional life as an analytical research consultant, working primarily in the biotechnology and pharmaceutical industries on research issues related to mental health. He holds an affiliate faculty appointment at the University of Washington School of Medicine in its Department of Bioengineering, where he has been named Outstanding Faculty of the Year at the College of Engineering, the Merrill Dow/Continuing Medical Education National Teacher of the Year, and twice, the Bioengineering Student Association Teacher of the Year.

Medina was the founding director of the Talaris Research Institute, a Seattle-based research center originally focused on how infants encode and process information at the cognitive, cellular, and molecular levels. Medina's books include the *New York Times* best-seller *Brain Rules,* the national best-seller *Brain*

Rules for Baby, Brain Rules for Aging Well, The Clock of Ages, Depression, What You Need to Know About Alzheimer's, The Outer Limits of Life, Uncovering the Mystery of AIDS, The Genetic Inferno, and *Of Serotonin, Dopamine and Antipsychotic Medications.* He has produced numerous courses on brain function, including a 24-lecture set for The Great Courses Company called *Your Best Brain.* He has also worked as a consultant to the Education Commission and speaks regularly on the relationship between cognitive neuroscience and education.

Related ASCD Resources

At the time of publication, the following resources were available (ASCD stock numbers in parentheses):

PD Online® Courses
The Brain, Memory, and Learning Strategies, 2nd Edition (#PD11OC112M)
Understanding Student Motivation, 2nd Edition (#PD11OC106M)

Print Products
Brain Matters: Translating Research into Classroom Practice, 2nd Edition by Patricia Wolfe (#109073)
Brain-Based Teaching in the Digital Age by Marilee Sprenger (#110018)
Managing Your Classroom with Heart: A Guide for Nurturing Adolescent Learners by Katy Ridnouer (#107013)
The Power of the Adolescent Brain: Strategies for Teaching Middle and High School Students by Thomas Armstrong (#116017)
Research-Based Strategies to Ignite Student Learning: Insights from a Neurologist and Classroom Teacher by Judy Willis (#107006)
Teaching Students to Drive Their Brains: Metacognitive Strategies, Activities, and Lesson Ideas by Donna Wilson and Marcus Conyers (#117002)
Teaching with the Brain in Mind, 2nd Edition by Eric Jensen (#104013)

For up-to-date information about ASCD resources, go to www.ascd.org. You can search the complete archives of *Educational Leadership* at www.ascd.org/el.

ASCD myTeachSource®
Download resources from a professional learning platform with hundreds of research-based best practices and tools for your classroom at http://myteachsource.ascd.org/

For more information, send an e-mail to member@ascd.org; call 1-800-933-2723 or 703-578-9600; send a fax to 703-575-5400; or write to Information Services, ASCD, 2800 Shirlington Road, Suite 1001, Arlington, VA 22206 USA.